The Big Little Devotional Guide

SERIES 1

Little
WORSHIP
Company

With thanks to Tim Dobson, Sarah Joy, Colse Leung, Rachel Noyce, Jo Sunderland and Jenny Sykes.

Additional images by Sarah Joy, Ramsey Selim, Jo Sunderland and Shutterstock.

Contents

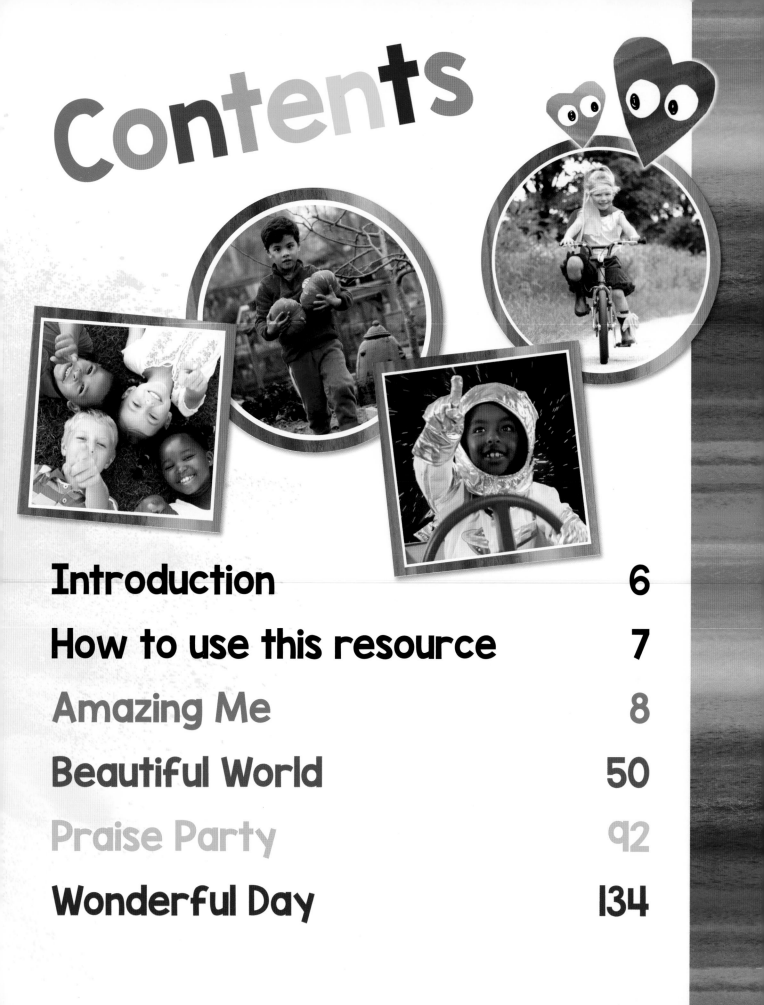

Little WORSHIP Company

Discovering GOD together

At **Little Worship Company,** our heart is to inspire and delight children with a knowledge of God, and to support them as they begin to take their first steps of faith. We also want to help parents as they walk with their children on this wonderful journey. Our range of beautifully-crafted, Biblically-based resources have been designed with the whole family in mind, so that all God's children, little ones and bigger ones, can discover more of God and His incredible love together.

There are four stunning DVDs that make up **Little Worship Company** Series 1:

- **Amazing Me**
- **Beautiful World**
- **Praise Party**
- **Wonderful Day**

This devotional guide has been written for use alongside the complete Series 1. In this book, you and your family are invited to journey with our hosts, Hal and Mr. and Mrs. Looyah, as they discover God and His amazing love for us together.

Welcome to the Big Little Devotional Guide!

This devotional guide has been divided into four sections, for use alongside the **Little Worship Company** Series 1 DVDs.

Amazing Me

We are all God's children, made and loved by our Heavenly Father. In **Amazing Me**, you'll explore how special we are – discovering not only the amazing people we were made to be, but the even MORE amazing God who invites us to be His friends.

Beautiful World

Our world is amazing! **Beautiful World** leads you and your family on a journey through the Bible's creation story, inspiring wonder in the incredible world we live in and helping us to see the God who made, knows and loves it – and who made, knows and loves us too.

Praise Party

Everyone loves a party – and the best ones of all are praise parties! **Praise Party** helps us to understand what it means to praise and worship God, not only with singing, dancing and instruments, but with our hearts, feet and hands too – to keep us praising God in every season of our lives.

Wonderful Day

The Bible is full of God's good promises to us. **Wonderful Day** helps you and your family to explore what these mean for us today, from the moment we wake up until we go to bed – and what it means for us to love and live for God each day in turn.

How to use this resource

To make the most of this resource, choose a time of the day or week which suits you and your family. It might be just before bed, just after lunch or sometime over the weekend.

- **Watch a chapter from the DVD.** Each chapter will include a short slot from Hal and a worship song.

- **Read through the accompanying Bible verse** and short, family-friendly reflection, found in this devotional guide.

- **As a family, talk through the discussion question together.** Close with the short prayer found at the bottom of the page.

Each reflection includes a simple craft or recipe suggestion to go with it. You could do this as part of the reflection, or at another time to remind you of some of the ideas you've been exploring.

What else is in this resource?

As well as all-age devotions, you'll find a little 'big' thought that draws on the same themes but is aimed specifically at adults. Each one includes suggestions for further reflection and a short prayer. This could be something you reflect on while your child engages in the craft, or you might choose to read it over a cup of tea, by yourself, later on.

At **Little Worship Company**, we want to provide you with practical ideas for making your faith part of family life. Throughout these pages, you'll find some of our best ideas for discovering God together in daily life – from tried and tested tips for connecting with God during this busy life season, to family-friendly ways of finding wonder in God's world.

Old or young, big or small –
every single one of us is precious to God!

You'll probably spot a few LOVE BUGS on our pages. They might be little – but they remind us of God's BIG love for us.

Amazing Me

God made me

Psalm 139:13-14 (LWC)

You created every single tiny bit of me.
You put me together in my mummy's tummy.
Thank you God.
I am brilliantly and marvellously made.

Wow! Did God really make me?

Yes, Hal, He did. He made you and He knows you inside and out!

Have you ever seen a mummy with a baby in her tummy? You can't really see the baby – just a bump which the baby snuggles inside! But the Bible says that God has always seen us and always known us – even before we were born! In fact, the Bible says that God is the one who made us. He put us together, like an artist making an amazing piece of art.

He knows every single thing about you. The colour of your eyes and your hair, the things you are really good at, even the things that make you laugh and cry – He made and knows it all. You are God's special creation – **His fantastic, one-of-a-kind work of art!**

TALK TOGETHER

Talk about all the things which make you one of a kind. Say thank you to God for them!

MAKE TOGETHER

You are God's work of art. Take some play dough. You might like to make a little person, or a collection of people, like your family and friends. As you do it, think about how God carefully made you – and smiled as He did so! Model a little heart and put it in the middle of your play-dough people to show how much God loves you!

PRAY TOGETHER

Dear God, **thank you that I am one of Your amazing ideas!** Thank you that You know every single part of me and that I am incredibly special to You. **Amen.**

Amazing Me

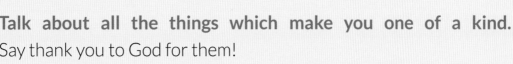

TIME TO REFLECT

Psalm 139:13-18

For you created my inmost being; you knit me together in my mother's womb.

I praise you because I am fearfully and wonderfully made;

your works are wonderful, I know that full well.

My frame was not hidden from you when I was made in the secret place,

when I was woven together in the depths of the earth.

Your eyes saw my unformed body; all the days ordained for me

were written in your book before one of them came to be.

How precious to me are your thoughts, God! How vast is the sum of them!

Were I to count them, they would outnumber the grains of sand –

when I awake, I am still with you.

"In the beginning, God created..." These are the very first words in the Bible and they set the tone for the rest of Scripture. God is the author of life, the first and last, Alpha and Omega. He is inextricably linked to all created things – and that includes us. This magnificent psalm is all about how our lives, our very selves, are intimately bound up in God. Whether we feel it or not – even whether we choose it or not! Our lives have been in God's hands from the moment we were conceived. And they still are. There

is no place we can go which is beyond His reach. There is no part of us which is beyond His understanding. He knows our secret thoughts, our hopes and fears, our joys and sorrows too – and He is with us in all of it.

THIS PSALM OVERFLOWS WITH JOY AND THANKSGIVING – AND WITH GOOD REASON.

We can find freedom in being known and held by the God who made us. As parents, we can be encouraged that this is true for our children too. There are no words to describe seeing your child face-to-face for the first time, or what it's like to watch them grow and to discover their emerging personalities. But there is so much we don't know about them yet – which can bring excitement and fear in equal measure! But God knows them. They are His own precious creation. He has them in His hands, just as He has us in His hands. And we can be completely confident that He will not let any of us go.

TIME TO ACT

1   Read the following words from Psalm 139:14:
I praise you because I am fearfully and wonderfully made.

Read them several times, emphasising each of the words in turn, for example:

I praise you because I am fearfully and wonderfully made.

I praise you because I am fearfully and wonderfully made.

I praise you because I am fearfully and wonderfully made.

What might God be saying to you through this?

2   Look back over any pictures you've collected of your child(ren), from their earliest days until now. As you look at them, reflect on God's perfect knowledge of you and your family and commit yourselves to Him.

TIME TO PRAY

I praise you, God, because You have known and loved me from the very beginning of my life.

Thank you that Your hands are big enough to hold me, my family and every single person in this world, and that we can trust You completely.

Amen.

60 SECONDS

ONLY GOT A MINUTE?

- God is the author of life, the first and the last.

- Our lives have been in God's hands from the moment we were conceived. He still holds us.

- God holds our children, just as He holds us.

- He will not let us go.

BIG

Amazing Me

God made me – I'm His amazing work of art!

1 Peter 2:9 (LWC)

I am God's very special treasure.

Yes you are, Hal. But not only that. God LOVES YOU too – more than you could ever imagine!

What is your number one, most favourite thing in the world? A teddy? A toy train? A blanket? Maybe it's your family? We all have something that we like to keep close to us – something that's really special to us. And God does too. **You!**

The Bible says that you are God's special treasure. He made you, He knows you, and **He really, really loves you!** In fact, there's nothing in the world more precious to Him than you. The Bible calls God our amazing Heavenly dad who is always beside us. He carries us when we get tired. He hugs us when we feel sad. And there's nothing in the world that can ever stop Him from loving us.

TALK TOGETHER

Collect up your most special things. Take some time to play with them. Or maybe have a big cuddle with your mum or dad! How does it make you feel? Think about how God feels the same way about you – but even more!

MAKE TOGETHER

You are God's precious child. Make a finger puppet family using pipe cleaners, pom-poms for the heads and googly eyes. Think about how you are part of God's family, loved by an amazing Heavenly Father!

PRAY TOGETHER

Dear God, **thank you that I am Your special treasure** and You are my Big Heavenly Dad. Thank you that You are with me and that You love me more than I will ever know. **Amen.**

Amazing Me

TIME TO REFLECT

John 1:1-13

In the beginning was the Word, and the Word was with God, and the Word was God. He was with God in the beginning. Through him all things were made; without him nothing was made that has been made. In him was life, and that life was the light of all mankind. The light shines in the darkness, and the darkness has not overcome it.

There was a man sent from God whose name was John. He came as a witness to testify concerning that light, so that through him all might believe. He himself was not the light; he came only as a witness to the light.

The true light that gives light to everyone was coming into the world. He was in the world, and though the world was made through him, the world did not recognize him. He came to that which was his own, but his own did not receive him. Yet to all who did receive him, to those who believed in his name, he gave the right to become children of God – children born not of natural descent, nor of human decision or a husband's will, but born of God.

It's said that an eminent theologian was once asked what was the most important lesson He'd learned over the years. His answer was simple:

"JESUS LOVES ME – THIS I KNOW, FOR THE BIBLE TELLS ME SO."

One of the big themes that runs through Scripture is God's incredible love for the world He created. And that love is supremely expressed in Jesus. It's often said that something is worth what somebody is willing to pay for it. We know how precious we are to God because He was willing to send His Son to die for us – to deal, once and for all, with the sin that separated us from Him and to welcome us into His family. Yes, Jesus loves us. The cross proves it.

Becoming a parent teaches you new lessons in love. You discover what it means to give happily and forgive readily, to rejoice in the hugs and little expressions of love, and to sacrifice without counting the cost. As we learn, first-hand, what it means to love like this, let's not forget that we, too, are children of a Heavenly Father, dearly beloved by the One who initiated and perfected it. This news is almost too wonderful to grasp. There are so many pictures that Scripture uses for God – Creator, Judge, Master. But God's heart is that we know Him intimately, as we know a parent. The love we have for our children helps us understand His love for us, but it still falls short. God really delights in us – despite our weaknesses and failings. He doesn't run out of patience when we get it wrong. And He is always at hand to help us – we only need to ask!

TIME TO ACT

1 When are the times you need to be reassured of how precious you are to God? Take some time to meditate on the words of this hymn:

How deep the Father's love for us
How vast – beyond all measure –
That He should give His only Son
To make a wretch His treasure.

Stuart Townend © 1995 Thankyou Music

2 How have you changed since becoming a parent? How has your relationship with God changed since becoming a parent?

Take some time to read and reflect on 1 John 3:1:

See what great love the Father has lavished on us, that we should be called children of God! And that is what we are!

Think about what you long to be for your children; and consider how God is all of this and more to them, and to you too.

TIME TO PRAY

Thank you, God, that even though I am fully grown, I am still Your child.

May I learn to be loved by You, and love like You in turn.

Amen.

ONLY GOT A MINUTE?

- God loves the world He created.

- We are so precious to God.

- The love we have for our children helps us begin to understand God's love for us – but His love for us is deeper, bigger and perfect.

- God delights in us, despite our weaknesses and failings.

- God's love never runs out.

Amazing Me

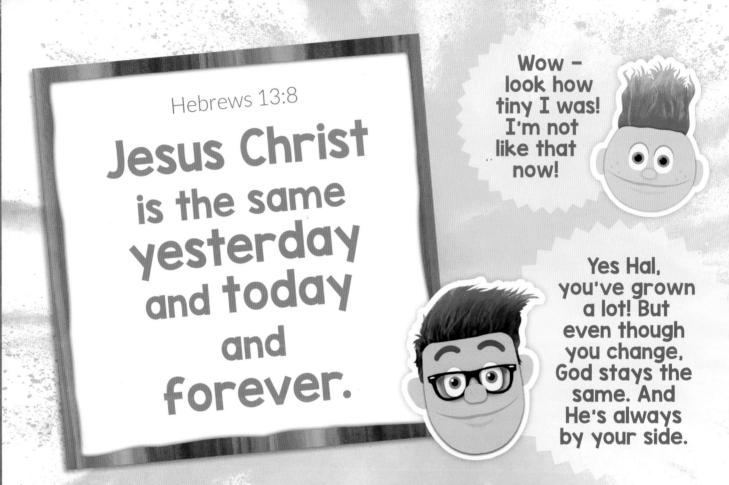

Hebrews 13:8

Jesus Christ is the same yesterday and today and forever.

Wow – look how tiny I was! I'm not like that now!

Yes Hal, you've grown a lot! But even though you change, God stays the same. And He's always by your side.

Do you remember what you were like as a baby? You gurgled and babbled. You wiggled your arms and waggled your feet. You played with rattles and baby toys. But now you are bigger. And you are so different. You can use lots of grown up words. You don't have a rattle any more – you play with bigger children's toys now. Maybe you can ride a bike, or even write your name!

You will change a lot as you grow. But even though you change, God doesn't. The Bible says that God is the same, every day and for evermore. This means that we can completely trust His promises to us. Because He doesn't change, **we know that God will always be with us and always, always love us!**

TALK TOGETHER

God will always be our friend. What do you think makes somebody a good friend? How is God a good friend to us?

MAKE TOGETHER

We might change, but God always stays the same. Make a clock out of a paper plate, a couple of cardboard hands and a paper fastener. A grown-up can help you to write the numbers on it or you can use stickers. Remember that, as time goes by, God will always be there for you.

PRAY TOGETHER

Dear God, **thank you that even though I will change, You never will.** Thank you that You will be with me as I grow and that You will always be my best friend. **Amen.**

Amazing Me

TIME TO REFLECT

Hebrews 13:8

Jesus Christ is the same yesterday and today and forever.

Is there a crazier time of life than when you become a parent? There are so many pressing demands, twenty-four hours a day, seven days a week. No two days are the same. You're in a constant state of flux, with routines changing from one week to the next. In fact, everything seems to be changing. Our core sense of identity and purpose changes dramatically. We become this brand-new person, 'Mummy' or 'Daddy' – something that is both a huge privilege and a huge responsibility! And during this particularly intense season, our walk with God may also change. We may find we struggle to connect with God in the ways we used to. Regular quiet times and church in the sanctuary (rather than the crèche) are not always possible. When our lives are so bound up with our children and their needs, creating dedicated space for God becomes a real challenge.

AS EVERYTHING AROUND US CHANGES, IT'S ENCOURAGING TO REMEMBER THAT GOD NEVER WILL.

His love for us is never in question, based as it is on His perfect nature rather than our imperfect devotion. And His plans, purposes and promises are just as unchanging. As new parents we can sometimes feel a bit lost – personally and spiritually. But the eternal, unchanging God is doing a new thing. He is always opening new ways of encountering Him and His goodness, providing new opportunities to serve and glorify Him. This busy season of early parenthood is like nothing else. But we can be confident that God is as present in our lives now as He ever was, walking beside us and leading us forward.

TIME TO ACT

1   Think about all the different ways you encountered God before you had children. Do you find it easy or difficult to do this now you are a parent? Ask God to show you new opportunities and rhythms for connecting with Him daily during this busy season.

2   We need to be intentional about spending time with the people we love – including God! Book a few hours in the diary to have some 'soul space' – whether that's through a long prayer walk or run, reading the Bible or going to a worship event. If finding childcare is difficult, why not consider setting up a child-minding triplet within your church and taking it in turns?

ONLY GOT A MINUTE?

- As everything around us changes, it's encouraging to remember that God never will.

- His plans, purposes and promises are unchanging.

- God is offering us new ways to encounter Him. Look for them.

TIME TO PRAY

Thank you, Father, that even though we may change, You are always the same.

In all the busyness of my life right now, help me to see You more clearly, love You more dearly and follow You more nearly each and every day.

Amen.

- Be confident that God is as present in our lives now as He ever was, walking beside us and leading us forward.

Amazing Me

"When we come to the end of ourselves, we come to the beginning of God."

Billy Graham

Draw near to God
THE BUSY PARENT'S GUIDE TO CONNECTING WITH GOD

Life with small children is incredibly busy. And that's putting it mildly. It can be difficult to find space for God when you're faced with a thousand pressing demands from the moment you wake up to last thing at night. (And, if your kids don't sleep, throughout the night as well!) But God is never far away. Some of these ideas might help you to become aware of Him with you, even on the busiest days.

- **Have conversations with God.** You might think of Him walking beside you as you push a buggy or sitting beside you at the office. Take a moment to talk over anything that's on your mind. Picture Jesus sitting with you and your family at the dinner table. What conversation would you like to have with Him? How would He include all the family?

- **Say thank you often.** Being thankful for all we've been given increases our awareness of the One who gives it. Whether it's the sight of blossom in spring, or a safe journey, give thanks to God throughout the day.

- **Mind the 'gaps'.** It's possible to combine daily, routine tasks with opportunities to connect with God. Play and sing worship songs around the house. Listen to audio versions of the Bible in the car. Play a study podcast while you prep the vegetables. Sing worship songs or whisper Bible verses over your children as you settle them to sleep.

- **Pray through the chores.** Many of the things we do each day can remind us of God's work in our lives. Pray for your children as you sort their laundry. Thank God for His forgiveness as you clean up messy plates and worktops. Remember how God promises to work all things together for good every time you compost your vegetable waste.

- **Make space for silence.** Sometimes all we need is time to rest. Even if it's just once a day, invest five minutes in doing nothing. Let the next urgent thing wait and find God's peace in the midst of the busyness.

- **Journal.** Keep a record of any 'God' words people have said or given to you, or places where You've experienced His goodness. Look back over it regularly and use it to praise God. Why not do this as a family?

- **Get appy.** With all this technology literally at our fingertips, why not use it to connect with God? Download Bible-reading apps, or apps that will help you pray. Use them when you have a spare minute.

- **Keep an eye on God's promises.** Stick up God's promises or favourite Bible verses around the house. Why not turn the fridge into a prayer-and-promise-wall?

- **Get out more.** Walking gives you space to think – as well as a chance to enjoy God's beautiful world. Why not go on a 'wonder walk' with your family? What will you see to make you say "wow"?

Amazing Me

1 Timothy 4:12 (MSG)

Don't let anyone put you down because you're young.

When will I be old enough to be God's friend? When I'm eight? Or maybe twelve?

Oh, Hal! You're never too young to know God! You can be friends with Him right now!

"You can't go on the zipwire. You're too small!"

"You can't go in the big pool. You're too small!"

"You can't go to school. You're too small!"

It's true that you might be too small for some things. But there's one thing you're never too little for: being God's friend!

The Bible is full of examples of God asking children to be His friends – like Samuel in the Old Testament and the little boy with his packed lunch in the New Testament. And Jesus always, always had time to talk to children! That's because you might be small, but you are incredibly important to God. **And you're never too young to learn how to listen to God and follow Him.**

TALK TOGETHER

If you have a children's Bible, **look up the story of God calling Samuel** and read it together (it can be found in 1 Samuel 3:1-10). Can you imagine how Samuel felt? How can we hear God speaking to us?

MAKE TOGETHER

You are so special to God! Make a crown out of cardboard and sparkly jewel stickers. Thank God that you are a very important person to Him!

PRAY TOGETHER

Dear God, **thank you that I am never too small to be Your friend!** Help me to keep my eyes open to see You, and my ears open to hear what You are asking me to do. **Amen.**

TIME TO REFLECT

1 Samuel 3:1-10

The boy Samuel ministered before the Lord under Eli. In those days the word of the Lord was rare; there were not many visions. One night Eli, whose eyes were becoming so weak that he could barely see, was lying down in his usual place. The lamp of God had not yet gone out, and Samuel was lying down in the house of the Lord, where the ark of God was.

Then the Lord called Samuel. Samuel answered, "Here I am."
And he ran to Eli and said, "Here I am; you called me."
But Eli said, "I did not call; go back and lie down." So he went and lay down.

Again the Lord called, "Samuel!"
And Samuel got up and went to Eli and said, "Here I am; you called me."
"My son," Eli said, "I did not call; go back and lie down."

Now Samuel did not yet know the Lord: the word of the Lord had not yet been revealed to him.

A third time the Lord called, "Samuel!"
And Samuel got up and went to Eli and said, "Here I am; you called me."
Then Eli realised that the Lord was calling the boy. So Eli told Samuel,
"Go and lie down, and if he calls you, say, 'Speak, Lord, for your servant is listening.'"
So Samuel went and lay down in his place. The Lord came and stood there, calling as at the other times,
"Samuel! Samuel!" Then Samuel said, "Speak, for your servant is listening."

This season of early parenthood opens up new possibilities of encountering God. It also opens up new opportunities for serving God. Parenting is itself a tremendous ministry given by God. He has entrusted you with a wonderful child that He made and loves. This child will encounter that love – initially – through you. From providing food, warmth and shelter, to showering smiles and kisses on your little one, you are – for now – the human face of God's care and provision. But, as well as meeting our child's physical and emotional needs in these early, formative years, we are invited to support our child's spiritual needs too, by helping them discern God's presence in their lives.

As parents we may hope and pray that our children will know and love God as they grow older. But how often do we think about them having a spiritual life now?

DO WE SEE HOW GOD IS ALREADY AT WORK IN OUR CHILDREN?

The Bible makes it clear that age is no barrier to knowing God and being used by Him. In the Old Testament, Samuel is called to an important priestly ministry as a mere child. Paul's instructions to Timothy show how he has complete faith in his (much younger) colleague to continue an important ministry amongst the church in Ephesus while he's away. Our children are never too young to walk with God. But they will need our help as they take their first steps on the journey. Like the priest Eli, we need to be alert to what God is doing, so we can help our children to recognise God as He calls to them.

TIME TO ACT

1 As you pray for your children, ask that God will help you to discern ways in which He is speaking to and leading your children.

2 We can encourage our children to walk with God for themselves by developing 'holy habits'. Think about how you build in prayer, Bible study and worship at home, so that God is not seen as belonging to Sunday but with you in your everyday lives.

TIME TO PRAY

Thank you, God,
that You love my child even more than I do,
and that you have tremendous plans for them.

Help me to see what You are doing in their life already and who You are shaping them to be.

Amen.

ONLY GOT A MINUTE?

- Parenting is a God-given ministry.
- Our children are never too young to walk with God.
- We can help our children to take their first steps on their faith journey.
- How can you build prayer, Bible study and worship with your child into your everyday routine?

Amazing Me

Ephesians 2:10 (LWC)

We are God's best artwork!

Wow! God made me!

That's right, Hal. And He knows exactly what you were made for: an amazing adventure with Him!

Birds were made to fly. Fish were made to swim. Cars were made to take people to exciting places. And ice cream was made to taste delicious on a sunny day. All kinds of wonderful things have been made to do all kinds of wonderful stuff. And we were too!

The Bible says that we are God's marvellous invention. He made us to do amazing things for Him – things that will change the world! We can find out about God's big ideas for us in the Bible. It's God's special instruction book for our life. We might not know exactly what God has planned for us as we get bigger, but if we look in the Bible we'll know which way to go!

TALK TOGETHER

What are your favourite inventions? What would you like to invent? Think about the kinds of things God created us to do – for example, helping other people.

MAKE TOGETHER

God has made you for an amazing adventure with Him! Make a pair of binoculars out of a couple of empty kitchen rolls, sticky tape and string or ribbon. To decorate them, wrap them with wool, paint them, use wrapping paper or add stickers. As you look through them, remember that God shows us the best way to go!

PRAY TOGETHER

Dear God, **thank you that You made me and that You really, really love what You made!** I can't wait to find out what You have planned for me! **Amen.**

Amazing Me

TIME TO REFLECT

Ephesians 2:1-10

As for you, you were dead in your transgressions and sins, in which you used to live when you followed the ways of this world and of the ruler of the kingdom of the air, the spirit who is now at work in those who are disobedient. All of us also lived among them at one time, gratifying the cravings of our flesh and following its desires and thoughts. Like the rest, we were by nature deserving of wrath. But because of his great love for us, God, who is rich in mercy, made us alive with Christ even when we were dead in transgressions – it is by grace you have been saved. And God raised us up with Christ and seated us with him in the heavenly realms in Christ Jesus, in order that in the coming ages he might show the incomparable riches of his grace, expressed in his kindness to us in Christ Jesus. For it is by grace you have been saved, through faith – and this is not from yourselves, it is the gift of God – not by works, so that no one can boast. For we are God's handiwork, created in Christ Jesus to do good works, which God prepared in advance for us to do.

God made us. But He is also *remaking us.* The Bible teaches that we are not functioning fully as the Maker intended. And the reason for this is our sin. Just as a virus infects and devastates a program, so sin has infected our human nature, marring God's wonderful design. But God has a remedy: Jesus. His death destroyed the power of sin, and now God is working in us to restore us to all He originally planned. If we want to know what this looks like – again, Jesus provides the answer. Jesus embodied all that God has in mind for us – the perfect template of humanity. And now, by His Spirit, God is patiently transforming every part of us to be more like Him – from our inner life (our thoughts and attitudes) to our outer actions.

AS PARENTS, WE WANT THE VERY BEST FOR OUR CHILDREN. AND THE BEST LOOKS LIKE JESUS.

Jesus lies at the heart of everything God has for us and wants to do in us. One of the greatest things we can ever do for our kids is to introduce them to Jesus. We can do this by sharing His stories – of His life, death and resurrection. But the most important thing we can do is inspire a love for Him. To show them what it means to follow Him by living out the values He taught – of trust in God, generosity and love without boundaries. So much of what our children learn is 'caught' not 'taught'. And there is nothing more compelling for our children than our own hearts fully alive and open to all God is calling us to in Christ.

TIME TO ACT

1 We are God's amazing work of art – a masterpiece that He is still sculpting and shaping as we submit our lives to Him. Take some time to commit yourself to God again. Know that His Spirit is in you, guiding you and helping you to become more like Jesus.

2 As parents, we want the very best for our children. The best, ultimately, is to place Jesus front and centre of our home lives and to live for Him together. How will you demonstrate what it means to love Jesus – in the things you say and the things you do?

TIME TO PRAY

Thank you, God,
that I am your handiwork.

Thank you that by Your Spirit You are making me more like Jesus.

May You truly be Lord of my life and let me model that to my family.

Amen.

60 SECONDS

ONLY GOT A MINUTE?

- God made us. But He is also *remaking* us.

- By His Spirit, God is patiently transforming every part of us to be more like Him.

- To inspire our children and to introduce them to Jesus, we need to model our own love for God.

- How can you demonstrate what it means to love Jesus, in the things you say and the things you do?

BIG

Amazing Me

Zephaniah 3:17

He will take great delight in you...
He will rejoice over you with singing.

I really want to make God happy! But I know I don't always get it right.

Hal, God's love for you is SO big! Nothing will ever change how much He cares for you.

Think about your favourite toy. What would you do if it went missing? You'd look for it, of course! Under the bed, in cupboards, behind the sofa. You'd search everywhere. And when you found it? You'd be so happy! You'd jump and cheer. Maybe you'd do a jiggly, wiggly dance!

Sometimes, it's like we walk away from God. We don't listen to Him, or we make choices that upset Him or other people. And that makes God sad. But no matter what we do, He loves us just the same. He's so happy when we come back to Him and say sorry – just like you're happy when you find a missing toy! In fact, the Bible says **He's so excited that He sings a song over us to celebrate!**

TALK TOGETHER

It's not always easy saying sorry, but it's a really important thing to do. When are the times you need to say sorry to God or to other people?

MAKE TOGETHER

Nothing will ever stop God from loving us. Make a 'love bug' stained-glass window out of sheets of sticky-back plastic and little squares of tissue paper. Stick the tissue paper onto a sheet of plastic, then stick another sheet over the top. Cut it into the shape of a 'love bug' and stick it onto a window. When the sun shines through it, remember how much God loves you!

PRAY TOGETHER

Dear God, **I'm really sorry for the times I make bad choices.** Thank you that I'm Your precious child, and that there's nothing in the world that stops You from loving me. **Amen.**

Amazing Me

TIME TO REFLECT

Zephaniah 3:14-17

Sing, Daughter Zion; shout aloud, Israel!
Be glad and rejoice with all your heart, Daughter Jerusalem!

The Lord has taken away your punishment, he has turned back your enemy.
The Lord, the King of Israel, is with you; never again will you fear any harm.

On that day they will say to Jerusalem, "Do not fear, Zion; do not let your hands hang limp.
The Lord your God is with you, the Mighty Warrior who saves. He will take great delight in you;
in his love he will no longer rebuke you, but will rejoice over you with singing."

Is there a more beautiful picture than that of our Heavenly Father singing over His children? And yet this promise of tender, wonderful love is bigger than we can imagine. It comes towards the end of Zephaniah – a prophetic book painting God's people at their most rebellious and hard-hearted. They have done absolutely nothing to deserve God's love – and instead everything to deserve His punishment. Yet God opens the way to find His forgiveness, a way back into relationship with Him. And this is our story too. We don't deserve God's love. Our sin makes us unworthy. But the good news of the gospel is that God's love is bigger than our sin. In Jesus, God provided a way to receive His forgiveness. God's Son took our punishment, so that we could become sons and daughters in turn.

As we get older, we perhaps become more aware of our sinfulness – that we don't live up to our own standards, let alone God's. As parents, this sense is often heightened. We have high hopes of what kind of parent we will be. But every hasty word or impatient reaction shows us our shortcomings in high definition.

IT IS ENCOURAGING TO REMEMBER THAT WE ARE NOT DEFINED BY OUR SIN, BUT BY THE GRACE OF GOD.

He doesn't give up on us. His love never runs out. His mercies are new every morning. And when we truly discover God's incredible love for us, we will see grace at work in our lives and relationships. It's only as we humbly encounter God's forgiveness, kindness and patience with us that we find ourselves becoming more forgiving, kind and patient in turn.

TIME TO ACT

1   Reflect on this verse from 1 John:

This is the kind of love we are talking about – not that we once upon a time loved God, but that he loved us and sent his Son as a sacrifice to clear away our sins and the damage they've done to our relationship with God.

1 John 4:10 (The Message)

Take some time to confess to God. Unburden your heart of all your weaknesses and failings. Know that He rejoices in you and receive His forgiveness and grace.

2   Our lives are defined by God's grace. How can we demonstrate that grace in our homes and communities? What does it mean to model the grace of God in the way we speak about each other? And in our actions towards each other?

TIME TO PRAY

Search me, O God, and know my heart.

See if there is any offensive way in me, and lead me in the way everlasting.

Amen.

(Based on Psalm 139:23-24)

BIG

ONLY GOT A MINUTE?

- God's love is bigger than our sin and unworthiness.

- Through Jesus, God has created a way to forgive us and to take away our punishment.

- This means we are now children of God!

- When we are not perfect parents, remember that we are not defined by our own shortcomings, but by God's grace.

- God doesn't give up on us – His love never runs out.

And what does the Lord require of you?

To **act justly** and to **love mercy** and to **walk humbly** with **your God.**

Micah 6:8

"Point your kids in the right direction..."

Proverbs 22:6 (MSG)

DEVELOPING HOLY HABITS AS A FAMILY

It's amazing the things we can remember from our childhood. The things we hear and the things we do stay with us for the rest of our lives. As parents, we want our children to encounter God. And we have an incredibly important role in helping them to do this. Why not have a go at developing some of these 'holy habits' in your home?

- **Discover Jesus together.** Take time regularly to explore the gospel stories with your children. As you read them, talk about what Jesus is like. What lessons can we learn *about* Him? What can we learn *from* Him?

- **Give thanks regularly.** Light a candle for each person at the dinner table and encourage them to find something to say thank you for. Create a 'thankfulness jar'. When you've done something fun, write or draw what happened. Remember the great times together. Use the jar as an opportunity to praise God.

- **Introduce the dinner-time 'high/low'.** Name one thing from your day that was a 'high' and one thing that was a 'low'. Thank God for the 'highs' and pray for the 'lows'.

- **Plan to pray.** It can be difficult to know what to pray when you're on the spot! Why not make a family prayer schedule? On Mondays pray for cousins, on Tuesdays pray for friends, etc. Use it at mealtimes or bedtimes. Or create a 'prayer hat' that contains different things to pray for. Pull a few things out of the hat each day and pray for them.

- **Build in 'prayer moments'.** Take a minute to say grace at mealtimes. Why not include a 'God bless today' prayer as your children go out to nursery or school?

- **Make time to listen.** Practise 'listening' as well as 'talking' in prayer. Spend a minute lying down in silence to listen to God – then talk about what He said to you.

- **Have a 'Bible board' in the house.** Get a magnet board or a chalkboard. Put up a Bible verse each week – one that will remind you and your family of God's good promises. If your children are a little older, why not see if they can learn it by heart?

- **Talk about your faith.** Faith is caught as much as taught. Share what following God means to you and times God has answered your prayers, so that your children see how your faith impacts you in real life.

- **Be hospitable.** We're called to "practise hospitality" (Romans 12:13). Invite people to join you for a meal or family outing – whether that's your children's friends or an elderly neighbour.

- **Learn generosity.** Research local charities that you could support as a family. Go shopping for food to give to a food bank. Give away toys and clothes that your children have outgrown. Do these things together, so that your children learn how good it feels to give!

Joshua 1:9 (LWC)

Be **strong** and be **courageous**. Do not be **afraid** or **troubled**, for the Lord your God is **with you** wherever you go.

I don't always feel amazing. Sometimes I feel scared.

I know, Hal. We all have to do scary things sometimes! But remember – God is right beside you.

What's the biggest, scariest thing you've ever done? Perhaps you learnt to swim or ride a bike. Maybe you started at nursery or school, or moved house. Going somewhere for the first time and making new friends is one of the scariest things we do – even for grown-ups!

God has a big adventure in store for us. As we get bigger, He'll take us to new places and ask us to do new things. We might not always feel good enough or brave enough to do them. But the Bible promises that God is always with us. (Actually, there's nowhere in the world that God isn't!) He's super big and super strong. And because He promises to help us, we can be super-duper-brave!

TALK TOGETHER

Talk about times when you have needed to be brave. Are you facing anything now that you need to be brave for? Talk to God about it!

MAKE TOGETHER

God makes us brave! Create your own superhero costume using an old T-shirt. What will your superhero name be? Remember that God makes us braver than any superhero, because we know He is always with us.

PRAY TOGETHER

Dear God, **thank you that I never need to be scared,** because You're always with me. Thank you that You make me brave! **Amen.**

TIME TO REFLECT

Joshua 1:1-11

After the death of Moses the servant of the Lord, the Lord said to Joshua son of Nun, Moses' aide: "Moses my servant is dead. Now then, you and all these people, get ready to cross the Jordan River into the land I am about to give to them – to the Israelites. I will give you every place where you set your foot, as I promised Moses. Your territory will extend from the desert to Lebanon, and from the great river, the Euphrates – all the Hittite country – to the Mediterranean Sea in the west. No one will be able to stand against you all the days of your life. As I was with Moses, so I will be with you; I will never leave you nor forsake you. Be strong and courageous, because you will lead these people to inherit the land I swore to their ancestors to give them.

"Be strong and very courageous. Be careful to obey all the law my servant Moses gave you; do not turn from it to the right or to the left, that you may be successful wherever you go. Keep this Book of the Law always on your lips; meditate on it day and night, so that you may be careful to do everything written in it. Then you will be prosperous and successful. Have I not commanded you? Be strong and courageous. Do not be afraid; do not be discouraged, for the Lord your God will be with you wherever you go."

So Joshua ordered the officers of the people: "Go through the camp and tell the people, 'Get your provisions ready. Three days from now you will cross the Jordan here to go in and take possession of the land the Lord your God is giving you for your own.'"

Some of the most enduring stories in the Bible are adventure stories. But the heroes are rarely 'heroic'. Joshua leading God's people into the Promised Land is one such story. God made a covenant to Abraham that His descendants would have a land of their own. Moses led his people out of Egypt but went no further than the wilderness. Now, God tells Joshua that the time has come for them to claim their inheritance. Although we don't hear anything from Joshua himself, God's words indicate how he must have been feeling. The command to *"be strong and courageous"* appears three times in this short passage. Clearly Joshua listened to God with a wave of conflicting emotions: excitement that they are about to reach the Promised Land and sheer terror at the magnitude of the task ahead.

LIFE WITH GOD IS AN ADVENTURE.

As parents, we want to show our children what it means to follow where He leads. But truly following God requires courage. The things He asks aren't always easy. We might feel daunted by a lack of experience. Or the task in question might go against the cultural grain. A particular weak spot for us may be our children: will doing this impact negatively on them? But these five simple words in verse 9 – *"Have I not commanded you?"* – are a complete game-changer. When the God of the Universe asks something of us, He gives us His authority to do it. We can find the courage to go ahead. Not because of our own confidence, but because we can trust in God, His perfect commands and His unfailing promises.

TIME TO ACT

1   It's natural to feel fearful in the face of a challenge. The opposite of fear is faith: trusting in who God is and in what He has done. Make a list of the times God has been faithful to you. Keep it close to you. Read it whenever you need to be reminded of God's faithfulness.

2   As parents, we need to model taking steps of faith. Has God been asking you to take a step of faith recently? What has been holding you back? Ask God to open the doors and to give you the courage to walk through them.

TIME TO PRAY

Thank you, God, that I can stand on Your faithful promises and rest in Your perfect will.

Grant me the courage to follow where You lead, now and always.

Amen.

60 SECONDS

ONLY GOT A MINUTE?

- Life with God is an adventure.

- Sometimes following God requires courage.

- But when the God of the Universe asks something of us, He gives us His authority to do it.

- We can trust in God, in His perfect commands and in His unfailing promises.

- Which doors do you need to walk through? Ask God to give you the courage to walk through them.

Amazing Me

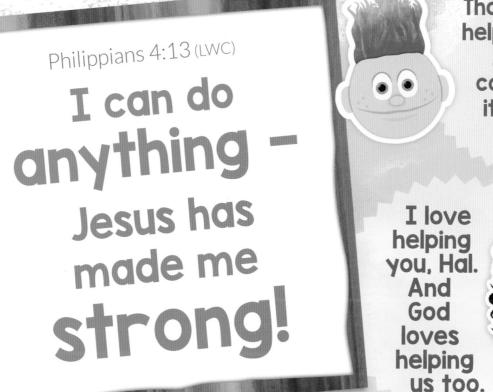

Philippians 4:13 (LWC)

I can do anything – Jesus has made me strong!

Thanks for helping me, Mum. I couldn't do it without you!

I love helping you, Hal. And God loves helping us too.

Some things are REALLY heavy! Think about a big box of your favourite toys. Or a suitcase full of clothes. There's no way we can carry these things by ourselves – we're just not strong enough! But the good news is – we don't have to. We have a grown-up around who will come and help us out!

As we get bigger, there might be times when our heart feels heavy. We might sometimes feel sad or worried. But the Bible promises that God is always near and always listening. There's nothing too big or too small for Him. And when we tell Him about it, He gives us His super-strength on the inside. **There's nothing we can't get through when we're with Him!**

TALK TOGETHER

Take some time to talk about anything which might be troubling you. Tell God about it. Ask Him to help you feel strong.

MAKE TOGETHER

God makes us strong. Make some handprints with paint. When they are dry, draw a picture of yourself in the middle to remind you that God carries you in His hands. Make some pictures for your family and friends too.

PRAY TOGETHER

Thank you, God, that **no matter what I go through, You will always help me.** Thank you that You make me strong! **Amen.**

TIME TO REFLECT

Philippians 4:4-13

Rejoice in the Lord always. I will say it again: Rejoice! Let your gentleness be evident to all. The Lord is near. Do not be anxious about anything, but in every situation, by prayer and petition, with thanksgiving, present your requests to God. And the peace of God, which transcends all understanding, will guard your hearts and your minds in Christ Jesus.

Finally, brothers and sisters, whatever is true, whatever is noble, whatever is right, whatever is pure, whatever is lovely, whatever is admirable – if anything is excellent or praiseworthy – think about such things. Whatever you have learned or received or heard from me, or seen in me – put it into practice. And the God of peace will be with you.

I rejoiced greatly in the Lord that at last you renewed your concern for me. Indeed, you were concerned, but you had no opportunity to show it. I am not saying this because I am in need, for I have learned to be content whatever the circumstances. I know what it is to be in need, and I know what it is to have plenty. I have learned the secret of being content in any and every situation, whether well fed or hungry, whether living in plenty or in want. I can do all this through him who gives me strength.

Life is rarely simple. Whether it's the everyday stresses and strains or more pressing trials and tribulations, life can often feel overwhelming. It is encouraging to remember, then, that large portions of the New Testament were written by people in difficult circumstances to people in similarly pressing situations. Paul wrote his letter to the Philippians during one of his many periods in prison – yet he's able to say with confidence, *"I can do all things through God who strengthens me."* He exudes peace, contentment and strength in all circumstances – even in times of extreme trial. There's a suggestion in verses 4-7 that this is as much a habit as a gift from God. It is the continual practice of trusting God – to provide and to see him safely through – that gives Paul this incredible peace.

We probably know by now that saying "yes" to following God does not guarantee us a trouble-free existence.

WHAT IT DOES PROMISE, THOUGH, IS KNOWING GOD, HIS PEACE AND HIS PRESENCE WITH US THROUGH IT ALL.

At these critical times, His strength becomes our strength. As parents, our instincts are to shield our children from life's difficulties, and there is definitely a place for this. We must exercise our judgment. But one of the greatest lessons we can teach our children is that when the going gets tough – and it will – God is with us, carrying us through it. We have a heavenly Father who loves us and who invites us to cast our burdens onto Him. It is not a sign of weakness to give God the things which we simply can't carry. It's the privilege of being His child.

TIME TO ACT

1   Reflect on these lines from an old hymn:

Oh, what peace we often forfeit!
Oh, what needless pain we bear!
All because we do not carry
everything to God in prayer.

Joseph M. Scriven

What concerns and troubles do you need to hand over to God today? Take them to Him and let His peace – the peace that passes understanding – wash over you.

2   As parents, we need to model what it means to trust in God in all circumstances. Consider your first response when life gets difficult. What place does prayer take? How can we encourage our children to pray with us in tough times?

TIME TO PRAY

Thank you, Father, that You are always with me.

Thank you that You are my strength when I have none of my own.

Help me to know Your peace and Your presence in all seasons and circumstances.

Amen.

ONLY GOT A MINUTE?

- Choosing to continually trust God in all circumstances gives us peace when times get tough.

- One of the greatest lessons we can teach our children is that when the going gets tough, God is there with us.

- It is not a sign of weakness to give God the things we can't carry. It's the privilege of being His child.

- What concerns and troubles do you need to hand over to God today? Take them to Him and let His peace fill you.

Amazing Me

Crafts and recipes

DEVOTION 1   PLAY-DOUGH FAMILY WITH HEARTS

How to make play dough:

- 8 tbsp plain flour
- 2 tbsp table salt
- 2 tsp cream of tartar
- 60ml warm water
- Food colouring
- 1 tbsp vegetable oil

1 Mix together in a bowl.

2 Once mixed, tip out onto a lightly flour-dusted surface and knead until smooth.

3 Store in an airtight container in the fridge.

DEVOTION 2

Finger puppet family

DEVOTION 3

Cardboard clock

DEVOTION 4

Cardboard crown

DEVOTION 7   SUPERHERO CAPE

You will need:

- An old T-shirt
- Fabric or marker pens
- Fabric or PVA glue
- Felt

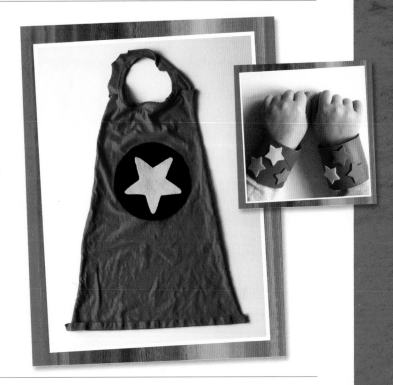

1. Get an adult to cut around the front of the neck of the T-shirt and then down the back sides to make a cape.

2. Decorate with fabric pens or marker pens.

3. Cut shapes out of the felt and stick on.

Why not use kitchen roll tubes to make matching armbands?

DEVOTION 5

Binoculars

DEVOTION 6

Stained-glass window

DEVOTION 8

Handprints

God holds me in his hands

Amazing Me

Amazing Me

thank you prayers

Thank you, God, for making me.

Thank you for my jumping legs.

Thank you for my strong arms.

Thank you for my listening ears.

Thank you for my blinking eyes.

Thank you for my nose that can smell.

Thank you for my full tummy.

Thank you for my cool hair.

Thank you for my HUGE smile.

Thank you, God, for amazing me!

Amen.

Beautiful World

Genesis 1:3 (MSG)

God spoke: "Light!" And light appeared.

Wow, Mum! The sky's turning red!

That's the sunset, Hal. I think it's God's way of showing us how beautiful and special the light is.

Do you have a light switch in your house? Or a night light by your bed? What happens when you switch it on? The room is filled with light! There are lots of things which give us light. Sunshine. Torches. Twinkly Christmas lights. We don't always think about light. But we notice when it's not there.

The Bible says that God made the world and the first thing He made was light. Light is really important to us. It helps us to see things – like all the amazing colours in the world. And that's not all. Trees and flowers need light to grow – and so do we! The sun's light keeps us healthy, happy and warm. Light is part of God's beautiful world. **Isn't God amazing?**

TALK TOGETHER

How many things can you think of that give light? How does light make you feel? Thank God for light every time you flick a light switch!

MAKE TOGETHER

God made light and colour. Get a piece of paper and make your own light picture. Drip poster paint on your picture (you may need to water it down) and blow it in different directions with a straw to make stars. If you mix in a small amount of PVA glue to the paint, then you can add glitter to make it sparkly too.

PRAY TOGETHER

WOW, GOD! Thank you for giving us light. Thank you for painting the world in different colours. Thank you that I can see and enjoy Your beautiful world. **Amen.**

DEVOTION 1 LIGHT OF THE WORLD

Beautiful World

TIME TO REFLECT

Genesis 1:1-5 *(read more in John 1:1-5, 9)*

In the beginning God created the heavens and the earth. Now the earth was formless and empty, darkness was over the surface of the deep, and the Spirit of God was hovering over the waters.

And God said, 'Let there be light,' and there was light. God saw that the light was good, and He separated the light from the darkness. God called the light 'day', and the darkness He called 'night'. And there was evening, and there was morning – the first day.

Genesis opens in darkness and nothingness. God is there, His Spirit hovering over the waters. And then He speaks those first, famous words: *"let there be light"*. Suddenly, the darkness is driven away and the stage is set for creation to follow.

It's impossible to overstate the importance of light to our world. It helps us see. It provides warmth and security.

FUNDAMENTALLY, LIGHT BRINGS LIFE.

Plants, which play such a critical role in our ecosystem, need light to grow and thrive. And we, too, need the sun's light in our bones and bodies to grow and thrive. Put simply – without light, we can't live.

The God of light, then, is the God of life. He is its source and sustainer. But it's clear from Scripture that the life God gives is more than just mechanical. As humans, we're born with an inbuilt sense that there's more to life than simply breathing, eating and sleeping. But what that 'something' is – that's been the source of endless debate, almost since time began. The Bible makes it clear that the answer is found in God. Throughout Scripture, God is associated with light – supremely in Jesus, the *"light of the world"* (John 8:12). His light shows us what's true – of God, of ourselves, of what the world is and of what it could be. It shows us which way we should go. And it overcomes the darkness – in ourselves, as well as in the world around us. In the beginning, God kick-started creation with His light. And as we live by the light of our marvellous Creator, so we can truly find life – and live it to the full.

TIME TO ACT

1 Write down the word 'light'. Spend a few minutes noting down everything that light makes you think of – whether that's what light does, or how it makes you feel.

Think about how Jesus called Himself the **_"light of the world"_** (John 8:12). How do your ideas about light help you to understand Jesus – who He is and what He does? Use these ideas to praise and thank Him.

2 In Matthew 5:14, Jesus called _us_ the light of the world. Look back over your list of 'light' ideas. How does it help you to understand what we are called to as Jesus' followers in the world?

TIME TO PRAY

God of light,
I praise You because You are everything I need.

Thank you that You are as constant as the sunrise, giving me light and life each new morning.

Amen.

ONLY GOT A MINUTE?

- When God says, **_"let there be light,"_** the darkness is driven away.

- Without light, we can't live.

- The God of light is the God of life, the source and sustainer of all things.

- Jesus is called the **_"light of the world"_** but He also called _us_ to be the light of the world. What might that mean?

Beautiful World

Jeremiah 31:35 (LWC)

God makes the **biggest** and best waves – listen to them **roar!**

Wow! Look at the ocean! It goes on forever!

Yep – it's big alright! But our God who made it is even BIGGER!

What's the biggest thing you've ever seen in your life? A house? A block of flats? A skyscraper? These are pretty big. But there are some amazing things in our world which are even bigger!

Think of mountains. They tower so high that they get lost in the clouds. In fact, the world's biggest mountain, Everest, is as tall as twenty skyscrapers stacked on top of each other! But that's nothing compared to the oceans. The Pacific Ocean is wider than *all* the countries of the world put together – and it goes so deep that if Mount Everest sat on the ocean floor, it still wouldn't reach the surface! But the Bible says that, as big as they are, God is even *bigger*. He made the mountains and the oceans. And He holds them *all* in His hands. **Isn't God amazing?**

TALK TOGETHER

Look at a map of the world or a globe together. Get a sense of how big the world is and the size of the oceans. Look up pictures of mountain ranges online. As you look at our huge world, remember that God is even bigger!

MAKE TOGETHER

God made the huge mountains and oceans. Make a mountain range collage. Cut up lots of triangles in different sizes and different shades of grey/black/brown. Stick them onto a piece of A4 paper so that they are overlapping to look like a mountain range. Colour the tops with white chalk to look like snow. Thank God for His amazing creations!

Why not ask a grown-up to write a Bible verse for you?

In one hand God holds deep caves... in the other hand he grasps the high mountains. *Psalm 95:4 (MSG)*

PRAY TOGETHER

WOW, GOD! Thank you for big mountains and enormous oceans! Thank you that You are bigger than all of them, and that You hold them – and me – in Your hands. **Amen.**

Beautiful World

TIME TO REFLECT

Genesis 1:6-10 (*read more in Mark 4:35-41*)

*And God said, 'Let there be a vault between the waters to separate water from water.'
So God made the vault and separated the water under the vault from the water above it.
And it was so. God called the vault 'sky'. And there was evening, and there was morning –
the second day.*

*And God said, 'Let the water under the sky be gathered to one place, and let dry ground appear.'
And it was so. God called the dry ground 'land', and the gathered waters he called 'seas'.
And God saw that it was good.*

For most of us, our experience of the sea is probably at the water's edge, enjoying gentle waves lapping on the shore. However, if you've been out on the ocean – especially in windy conditions – you'll appreciate something of its might. Throughout Scripture, the seas are seen as evidence of God's awesomeness. It's not just the size and scale of the oceans – although that would be enough. It's the oceans' power, their enormous waves truly terrifying to behold. In Biblical times, the seas inspired a healthy fear, and the God of creation even more so. His voice raised up the waves, and with a word He stilled them too. The seas were mighty – and their God was even mightier.

THE GOD OF THE OCEANS IS UNDOUBTEDLY POWERFUL. BUT SCRIPTURE REMINDS US THAT HE IS LOVING TOO.

There are several miracles in the Bible which involve God commanding the waters – for example, Moses and the Israelites crossing the Red Sea as they flee Egypt, or Joshua leading the people through the Jordan and into the Promised Land. In the gospels, Jesus and His friends are out on the Sea of Galilee when a sudden storm whips up the waves, leaving the disciples fearing for their lives. But a word from Jesus calms the storm – and the disciples' fearful hearts. This is something we must remember. The God we worship is almighty. Powerful. Strong. But that doesn't make Him aloof, or angry, or unfeeling. His might is tempered by His love, His power by His wonderful promises to us. The God of creation holds the oceans in His hands. But that's not all He holds – He holds us too.

TIME TO ACT

1 Psalm 46:10 says:

Be still and know that I am God.

Fill a bowl with water. Stir it around to make waves and then watch as it calms. As you do so, think about how God is mightier than the oceans. Invite His Spirit to give you His peace in whatever you might be experiencing.

2 Jesus said that our faith could move mountains (Matthew 17:20). It is not the strength of our faith as much as the size of our God that makes the difference. Talk to God about the challenges facing you, your church family and your nation. Is God asking you to take a step of faith in the midst of these?

TIME TO PRAY

God of the oceans,
I praise You for Your incredible power and for Your indescribable love.

Thank you that I have nothing to fear while You are beside me.

Amen.

ONLY GOT A MINUTE?

- God created the untameable oceans.

- His voice raised up the waves, and with a word He stilled them too.

- The seas are mighty, but our God is even mightier.

- The God of creation holds the oceans in His hands.

- God holds us in His hands too.

Beautiful World

Isaiah 55:12 (LWC)

The **mountains** and the **hills** will shout **loud songs** – and the **trees** **clap** their hands.

Wow! The trees are covered in flowers! They're amazing!

Yes, Hal. They are beautiful. And God made them all!

Have you ever seen juicy strawberries growing on a plant? Or shiny apples on a tree? Have you ever seen daisies and buttercups growing in the grass? If you have, then you'll know that all kinds of wonderful things grow out of the soil. And they were all made by God!

The Bible says that God filled the world with all kinds of growing things, from big, tall trees to bright, colourful flowers. They're not just beautiful to see and smell. They provide us with everything we need to live well – like food, shelter and even clean air. And not just us, but millions of animals, birds and insects too! Trees and plants are part of God's beautiful world. **Isn't God amazing?**

TALK TOGETHER

Go out into your garden or to the nearest park. Talk about the different things you can see growing there – trees, flowers, vegetables or grass. Or go to the fresh fruit and vegetable section of your supermarket. How many different types can you find? Say thank you to God for all the things you discover!

MAKE TOGETHER

God made all kinds of amazing trees and flowers! Make your own 3D daffodils. Cut out cardboard petals and use small yoghurt pots for the trumpets and lolly sticks for the stems.

PRAY TOGETHER

WOW, GOD! Thank you for tall trees and beautiful flowers. Thank you for juicy fruit and tasty vegetables. Thank you that You give us everything that we will ever need. **Amen.**

LITTLE

Beautiful World

TIME TO REFLECT

Genesis 1:11-13; 29-30

Then God said, 'Let the land produce vegetation: seed-bearing plants and trees on the land that bear fruit with seed in it, according to their various kinds.' And it was so. The land produced vegetation: plants bearing seed according to their kinds and trees bearing fruit with seed in it according to their kinds. And God saw that it was good. And there was evening, and there was morning – the third day.

Then God said, 'I give you every seed-bearing plant on the face of the whole earth and every tree that has fruit with seed in it. They will be yours for food. And to all the beasts of the earth and all the birds in the sky and all the creatures that move along the ground – everything that has the breath of life in it – I give every green plant for food.' And it was so.

The created world teaches us about the Creator. And the millions of wonderful things that spring from the soil speak volumes. God is a designer *par excellence*. The shapes, the sizes, the colours, the scents... they all reflect a designer with a flair for the spectacular. Not to mention the wonderful tastes. Any walk through a garden in bloom is a multisensory delight. But He's more than an artist. In this account of God's third day of creation, there's a small phrase which marks God out as a flawless engineer. It's not just that He made plants and trees. He made them 'seed-bearing'. In other words, as God created them, He put in them the ability to reproduce year on year, and in abundance.

This act of creation, so thoughtfully engineered, shows us a generous God. He loves to give – and give plentifully. But it also suggests something else. On the third day, God creates trees and plants. And then, on the sixth day, He gives them to the newly-created people, animals and birds so that they will have all they need to live. This goes beyond generosity. The traditional term for this is 'benevolence'. It literally means 'willing us good'. The trees and plants show a God who's been thinking of us since before we were even created and who is committed to our provision and care. We might wonder what God is like – whether He's really as good as the Bible makes out. But creation shows us it's true.

EVERY FRUIT-BEARING TREE AND SEED-BEARING PLANT LEAVES US IN NO DOUBT THAT THE GOD OF GROWING THINGS IS ROOTING FOR US.

TIME TO ACT

1   As you walk around your community, be mindful of the trees and plants you see. As you look at them, thank God for His beautiful creation and in His extraordinary care.

2   Good things grow in all seasons – even if we can't see them. Likewise, it's not always obvious to see what God is doing during our own 'winter' months – but we know that we can trust in His faithfulness and in His ability to work all things together for good.

Take some time to look back at the ways God has provided for and led you in the past – in the tough times as well as the good. Thank God for His care. Can these reflections encourage you in the present?

TIME TO PRAY

God of growing things,
I praise You for Your generosity and kindness.

Thank you that You give us everything that we need, in every season of our lives.

Amen.

ONLY GOT A MINUTE?

- The world around us teaches us that our God is generous.

- The beauty of creation shows us God's creativity.

- Seed-bearing plants and trees demonstrate God's commitment to our provision and care.

- Good things grow in all seasons – even if we can't see them.

- The God of all growing things is rooting for us.

What a **wildly wonderful world,** God! You made it all.

Psalm 104:24
(The Message)

What a wonderful world
ENJOYING GOD'S CREATION AS A FAMILY

Nothing beats going out and enjoying God's beautiful world!

Why not try a few of these with your family?

- **Go on a 'wonder walk'.** Go to the woods, the countryside or the seaside. Or simply walk about your own community. Be intentional about spotting the nature all around you. Why not turn it into a treasure hunt? Find something beginning with each letter of the alphabet, or in each colour of the rainbow.

- **Make the most of each season.** Walk through bluebell woods in spring. Pick blackberries in late summer – they grow everywhere, even in cities! Collect conkers in autumn. Make a snowman in winter.

- **Get growing.** Plant bulbs in pots or in the garden together and watch the flowers grow. Grow fruit and vegetables from seed. Start them off in pots on the windowsill, then plant them out as they get bigger. And then enjoy picking and eating them when the time comes!

- **Meet the animals.** Visit a farm, zoo, aquarium or even just a pet shop. Talk about what you like about the animals, birds or fish that you see there. Thank God for making them.

- **Dig a little deeper...** Dig up the soil in the garden to spot creepy crawlies. Go rock pooling at the seaside to search for tiny crabs and sea creatures. Look (from a safe distance!) into rivers – can you spot any fish swimming there?

- **Find out more!** There are so many wonderful nature programmes available on TV or online. Watch them together. Talk about what you see and thank God for His amazing creations! Go to the library and flick through nature books. What fun facts can you find out?

- **Go stargazing.** This is easiest in the winter when it gets dark earlier. On a clear night, get out sleeping bags and make warm drinks. Put on coats, hats and scarves. Lie down in the garden and look at all the different stars you can see.

- **Make nature art.** When you go out, pick up fallen leaves, feathers, sticks, seeds, petals... whatever you can find! Take them home and turn them into a nature collage. Make seaside art at the beach. Collect shells and seaweed and use them to make a picture in the sand.

Psalm 147:4-5 (LWC)

He knows how many **stars** there are.
He gives **names** to all of them.
God is great!

I can see a star! And another one! And another one!

Yes, Hal. There are more stars out there than we can count. But God knows how many there are. He made them!

Our world can feel like a pretty big place. But it's teeny tiny compared to space! We live on planet Earth. Our planet is just one, small part of a big, amazing universe. Look into the night sky and you can see other planets, moons and thousands of bright, shining stars.

Human beings have been studying space for a long, LONG time. However hard we try, we'll never know all there is to know about our universe. We don't even know how many stars there are – it's impossible to count them all! But God knows. He's the one that made them. The Bible says that He put the stars in the sky, one by one, and that He calls them by name. And He knows *your* name too! **Isn't God amazing?**

TALK TOGETHER

If it's a clear night, look up into the sky. Can you see the stars? Are any brighter than the rest? Think about how God knows how many stars are in the sky – and how He knows you too!

MAKE TOGETHER

God sees and knows the whole universe. Cut out cardboard stars and either make them out of different colours or cover them with silver foil. Hang them at different lengths on a coat hanger to make a mobile/decoration for your room.

PRAY TOGETHER

WOW, GOD! Thank you for the bright sun.
Thank you for the twinkling stars. Thank you that You know every bit of our universe – and that You know me too. **Amen.**

Beautiful World

TIME TO REFLECT

Genesis 1:14-19 *(read more in Psalm 8)*

And God said, "Let there be lights in the vault of the sky to separate the day from the night, and let them serve as signs to mark sacred times, and days and years, and let them be lights in the vault of the sky to give light on the earth." And it was so. God made two great lights – the greater light to govern the day and the lesser light to govern the night. He also made the stars. God set them in the vault of the sky to give light on the earth, to govern the day and the night, and to separate light from darkness. And God saw that it was good. And there was evening, and there was morning – the fourth day.

Humankind has long been fascinated by the Universe. For millennia, people have been gazing up into the night sky, studying the stars to seek answers to their big questions. In the last hundred years of human history this fascination has only increased, with moon landings and space probes opening up exciting possibilities for understanding life beyond planet Earth. And yet the Universe remains a mystery – the distant constellations a reminder of how much more there is to know and explore. Perhaps that's why it provides such inspiration in Scripture as a way of comprehending God's greatness.

THE UNIVERSE IS THE BIGGEST THING WE SEE – THE THING FURTHEST FROM OUR GRASP, INTELLECTUALLY AND PHYSICALLY. BUT GOD CREATED IT.

He put the stars in their place and He calls them by name. There is nothing God cannot do, and nothing He does not know.

But it's clear from Scripture that there's a bigger mystery out there than even the Universe – and that's God's love for us. *"When I consider your heavens, the work of your fingers,"* the psalmist writes, *"what is mankind that you are mindful of them?"* (from Psalm 8:3-4). The Hebrew word for 'mindful' speaks of God's attention and loving kindness. He sees us. He knows us. And there's more. The King James Version translates Psalm 8:4 as *"what is the son of man, that Thou visitest him?"* It's a word that reminds us how this great and awesome God put aside His splendour to become human like us. The God who knows the limits of the Universe knows our limits too. He understands our every thought and weakness. And this majestic God who brought about the entire Universe is still with us now.

TIME TO ACT

1 There's nothing like gazing into the night sky to make us aware of our own smallness and seeming insignificance. And yet we are precious to God. Take some time to praise God for His awesome love for us.

2 Cut out some star shapes to use in your prayers. Write on them the names of people you want to pray for and place them around the house. Remember that God knows them – that He knows their needs and He cares for them.

TIME TO PRAY

God of the Universe,
I praise You for Your greatness and majesty.

Thank you that nothing in all creation is hidden from Your knowledge or Your wonderful love.

Amen.

ONLY GOT A MINUTE?

- The Universe is the biggest thing we see. It is so large that it is incomprehensible, yet God created it.

- Our Father put the stars in their place and calls them by name.

- There is nothing God cannot do and nothing He does not know.

- The God who knows the limits of the Universe knows our limits too.

- This majestic God, who created the Universe, is with us.

BIG

Genesis 1:20 (MSG)

God spoke:
Swarm, Ocean, with fish and all sea life!

Birds, fly through the sky over Earth!

Wow! I wish I could swim through the ocean!

The oceans are full of amazing creatures – and God made them all!

Have you ever seen a goldfish in a tank? Perhaps you have one in your house, or you've seen some at a pet shop. They're just one kind of fish – but there are thousands and thousands more. The rivers and oceans are bursting with them. And they all came from God's amazing imagination!

The Bible says that God filled the oceans with all kinds of sea creatures – wobbly jellyfish, clever octopuses, graceful dolphins, mighty whales and many more! And that's not all He made. The Bible says that He filled the sky with birds of all shapes, sizes and colours – from little sparrows in the back garden to bright parrots in the rainforests. He made them all, and He loves them all. **Isn't God amazing?**

TALK TOGETHER

How many kinds of fish can you find around you? You could visit an aquarium, or even just your local pet shop or garden centre. What about birds? See how many different kinds of birds you can spot in your garden or local park. You could look at pictures of fish and birds online or in books. Which species do you like the best?

MAKE TOGETHER

God made all kinds of fish and birds. Make a bird feeder/fat ball for the birds. See instructions on **page 88.**

PRAY TOGETHER

WOW, GOD! Thank you for weird and wonderful fish in the sea. Thank you for bright birds with beautiful voices. Thank you for everything that You've made! **Amen.**

Beautiful World

TIME TO REFLECT

Genesis 1:20-23 *(read more in Matthew 6:25-33)*

And God said, "Let the water teem with living creatures, and let birds fly above the earth across the vault of the sky." So God created the great creatures of the sea and every living thing with which the water teems and that moves about in it, according to their kinds, and every winged bird according to its kind. And God saw that it was good. God blessed them and said, "Be fruitful and increase in number and fill the water in the seas, and let the birds increase on the earth." And there was evening, and there was morning – the fifth day.

The Universe declares God's majesty; the oceans declare His might. We see God's benevolence in the trees and flowers. Living creatures – fish, birds and animals – are equally wonderful: a credit to the amazing Creator who made them. But seen through the lens of Scripture, they also provide a case study in God's love for us. Take birds, for example. Jerusalem in Jesus' day was overrun with sparrows. These small, common birds were generally considered of very little value – a pair sold for a penny to the poor for use in the temple. Yet, when Jesus is trying to teach his disciples how much they matter to God, it's the sparrows he turns to. Small as they are, God cares for them. He has His eye on them. And, He says, you're worth so much more than they are (Matthew 10:29-31).

These words echo those in the Sermon on the Mount in Matthew 6:26. Consider the birds of the air, Jesus says. They don't worry about where their next meal is coming from – God feeds them. And the conclusion Jesus draws on both occasions is the same.

IF GOD CARES FOR THE BIRDS, HOW MUCH MORE WILL HE CARE FOR YOU?

It's a message that speaks right to the heart of us. Even on a good day, as we're floored by the wonder of creation, we can feel small and insignificant. And on a bad day, when we feel like life is just too much to cope with, we can feel alone and downright forgotten. But the birds remind us that we are neither. God knows each one of us. He knows our situation. He knows our needs. And we are more precious to Him than we can dare to dream.

TIME TO ACT

1 Jesus tells us that we don't need to worry about our material needs – food, clothes, etc. – because God provides. Claim God's promise. Ask Him now for anything that you need.

2 Take some time to pray for the needs of people in your family, community or even nation. Could you be the answer to their prayers?

TIME TO PRAY

God of the sparrows,
I praise You that nothing is too small for Your notice, and no one too small for Your care.

Thank you that You care for me more than I could ever imagine.

Amen.

ONLY GOT A MINUTE?

- Living creatures – fish, birds and animals – are all made by God.

- Jesus said, "If God cares for the birds, how much more will He care for you?"

- When we feel small and insignificant, the birds remind us we are neither.

- God knows each one of us.

- We are more precious to Him than we can dare to dream.

Genesis 1:24-25 (MSG)

God spoke... and there it was: wild animals... cattle... every sort of reptile and bug.

Wow! Imagine having a nose like an elephant, or a big, long neck like a giraffe!

The world is full of amazing animals. God has a BIG imagination!

How many animals do you know? Think about farm animals – can you name ten? What about jungle animals – can you name another ten? What about pets? The world is FULL of incredible animals, reptiles and insects. And God made all of them!

The Bible says that God filled the world with animals – big ones, small ones, fluffy ones and fierce ones. Cows, sheep, cats and dogs. Huge elephants, tiny mice, tall giraffes, wriggly caterpillars and many, many more! There are literally MILLIONS of different kinds of animals and insects on our planet – and that includes some we've not even discovered yet. But even though *we* don't know them all, God knows them and loves them. **Isn't God amazing?**

LITTLE

TALK TOGETHER

How many different animals can you find this week? You could visit a farm, or the zoo, or even just a pet shop. You could look up different animals from around the world online or in a book. Ask an adult to read out some facts about the different animals you find. Which are your favourites? Why? Are there any particular animals you'd like to see?

MAKE TOGETHER

God made the animals and the insects. Make a paper-chain caterpillar. Add some antennae using pipe cleaners or cardboard and stick on googly eyes. Or make insects out of kitchen rolls/pipe cleaners/googly eyes, etc.

PRAY TOGETHER

WOW, GOD! Thank you for amazing animals and creepy crawlies. Thank you for things that run and things that wriggle. Thank you for everything You've made! **Amen.**

Beautiful World

TIME TO REFLECT

Genesis 1:24-25 *(read more in John 10:1-10)*

And God said, "Let the land produce living creatures according to their kinds: the livestock, the creatures that move along the ground, and the wild animals, each according to its kind." And it was so. God made the wild animals according to their kinds, the livestock according to their kinds, and all the creatures that move along the ground according to their kinds. And God saw that it was good.

Of all the animals on our planet, one finds itself mentioned in the Bible more than any other: the humble sheep. And no wonder. This farmyard favourite has been a staple of civilisation for thousands of years. Many of the heroes of the Old Testament kept sheep: Jacob, Moses and David to name but three. Jesus himself spoke about sheep – most famously in Luke 15 and John 10. The ins and outs of shepherding would've been familiar to people in Biblical times. The shepherd collected his sheep in the morning. He'd lead them out to the green pastures nearby. He watched over them as they fed, protecting them from predators and finding any that wandered off. It provided the perfect image to describe God's relationship with His people, found throughout the Old Testament. *"The Lord's my Shepherd, I'll not want,"* sang David (Psalm 23:1), overwhelmed by God's committed care. *"We all, like sheep, have gone astray,"* said Isaiah (Isaiah 53:6), explaining humankind's tendency to wander and God's willingness to rescue.

But what's striking when Jesus talks about Himself as the Good Shepherd is not just His care. It's His intimacy. Contrary to popular opinion, sheep do not aimlessly follow the crowd.

IN BIBLICAL TIMES, THERE WAS A STRONG BOND BETWEEN A SHEPHERD AND HIS SHEEP. SHEPHERDS GAVE THEIR SHEEP NAMES, WHICH THEY KNEW.

And the sheep recognised their shepherd's voice, following when he – and only he – called. It's a picture of belonging – of being known and loved, and of knowing and loving in turn. We don't just worship a deity or serve a master. We don't just receive things from a bounteous benefactor. We belong to the One who calls us by name. And His love will never let us go.

TIME TO ACT

1   The prophet Isaiah writes:

He tends his flock like a shepherd: he gathers the lambs in his arms and carries them close to his heart; he gently leads those that have young.

Isaiah 40:11

During this busy season of life, as we carry our own young in our arms, think about what it means to be loved and carried by God.

2   In the Bible, Jesus is described as both the Lion of Judah and the Lamb of God. Write down what each of those pictures means to you. How does each one shape or challenge your idea of Jesus? What does it mean to follow one who is both a lion and a lamb?

TIME TO PRAY

O God my Shepherd,
I praise You because You know me
and call me by my name.

Thank you that I belong to You.

Help me to hear Your voice each day
and stay close to You in turn.

Amen.

ONLY GOT A MINUTE?

- God says we belong to Him, like sheep belonging to a shepherd.

- The shepherd names and knows his sheep.

- The sheep hear his voice and trust him.

- We belong to the One who calls us by our own name.

- His love will never let us go.

Beautiful World

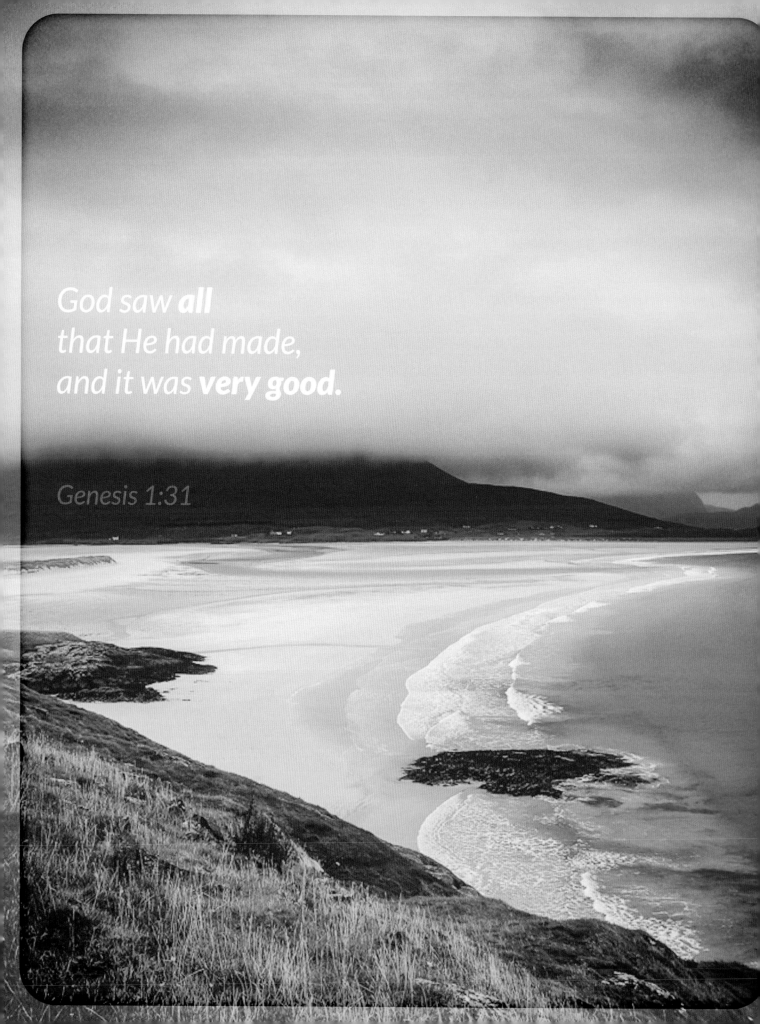

God saw **all** that He had made, and it was **very good.**

Genesis 1:31

Love God, love the planet
LEARNING TO LOOK AFTER GOD'S CREATION AS A FAMILY

"The earth is the Lord's, and everything in it." Psalm 24:1

God made a beautiful world – one that He loves completely. And He gave us the responsibility to look after it for Him (Genesis 1:28). Part of loving God, then, is learning to care for His wonderful creation. We're never too young to begin! Here are some easy ways to love God's lovely world:

- **Love your animals.** Encourage your children to be involved with looking after any family pets. Make a bird feeder **(page 88)** or a bug hotel for some of the creatures that visit your neighbourhood. Why not consider sponsoring an endangered animal?

- **Walk more.** Not only does walking help reduce harmful carbon emissions, it also encourages you to see the wonder in the world around you. Leave the car at home for short journeys. If walking for fun, why not litter pick at the same time?

- **Compost your vegetable waste.** Build a compost bin in the garden. This cuts down on waste going into the household bin, while enriching your soil in turn. Talk about your compost bin's favourite food: vegetable peelings, egg shells, tea bags… And make sure everyone takes a turn to feed it.

- **Shop second-hand.** This saves on waste, saves you money and may benefit a good cause. And, of course, it's always great to donate! Is there anything you could give away instead of throw away?

- **Use less energy.** As a family, get used to switching lights/the TV/toys off when they're not in use. Do the laundry at a lower temperature. (Maybe even do less laundry!) If you haven't done so already, and if it's possible, why not switch to a renewable energy supplier too?

- **Reduce what you get.** Try to avoid getting single-purpose items which can only go in the bin. Take your own bags to the shops. Make a weekly meal plan. Only buy food that you need and use up any leftovers.

- **Reuse what you have.** Before buying anything new – even stuff you 'need' – ask yourself if you have something else that would do the job. Old ice-cream tubs that will do for storage, clothes you forgot you had… You'll be amazed what you find you already have when you stop and think about it!

- **Recycle what you use.** Lots of household waste is now easily recycled. Why not teach children how to recycle by turning it into a game? Keep different boxes for plastics, cardboard, paper and aluminium. Time trial the children to see who can sort the recycling out the most quickly!

- **Buy ethically.** Pick up items that are fair trade, ethical, recycled or recyclable whenever possible. As a family, learn the different signs on the packaging and talk about what they mean. See if you can spot the signs at the supermarket.

Beautiful World

God made ME!

John 3:16 (MSG)

This is how much God loved the world: He gave his Son...

Wow! God made light, trees, fish, stars... and everything!

Yes, Hal. He made and loves it all. And there's something else He loves too – YOU!

The Bible says that God made this beautiful world and everything in it. But there was something really, really special that He had planned. Something that was even more amazing and even more wonderful than all the rest. **Us!**

God made us. And He loves us more than we can ever imagine. The Bible says that He loves us so much that He made Himself into a tiny human. He was born as a baby called Jesus. He came to live with us so that we could know Him better. And when He died, He made a special way for us to be friends with Him forever! God's love for us is bigger than the huge Universe He created. **Isn't God amazing?**

TALK TOGETHER

Talk about the people who are special to you. What do you love about them? Think about how you are special to God – and how much He loves you!

LITTLE

MAKE TOGETHER

God made us. He knows us – and He really, really loves us! Make some peg dolls. Using traditional wooden clothes pegs, draw a face and draw or add hair with wool. You can use pen to draw their clothes or use scraps of fabric to make skirts and tops. You can use pipe cleaners to make hands. As you do so, think how God made you, and how much He loves you!

PRAY TOGETHER

WOW, GOD! Thank you that You know me. Thank you that You love me. Thank you that, even though You are really, really BIG, You made Yourself into a teeny-tiny person so that I could be Your friend forever. **Amen.**

TIME TO REFLECT

Genesis 1:26-28 *(read more in John 15:9-17)*

Then God said, "Let us make mankind in our image, in our likeness, so that they may rule over the fish in the sea and the birds in the sky, over the livestock and all the wild animals, and over all the creatures that move along the ground."

So God created mankind in his own image, in the image of God he created them; male and female he created them.

God blessed them and said to them, "Be fruitful and increase in number; fill the earth and subdue it. Rule over the fish in the sea and the birds in the sky and over every living creature that moves on the ground."

God reveals something of Himself through all He's made. This includes His last creation. On the sixth day, Genesis tells us, God created people, and He made them *"in His image"*. God modelled us on Himself. Put another way – at the dawn of creation, God invested something of His divine character in us. It's true that sin has marred our humanity and we've fallen from God's ideal for us. But His likeness is still there. The very best parts of humanity are those which echo something of God our maker – such as goodness, truth or creativity. And without a doubt, it's love – freely and sacrificially given – that declares Him the loudest.

The Bible says that when we are in Christ, we are a new creation (2 Corinthians 5:17).

GOD IS UNDERTAKING A HUGE RESTORATION PROJECT IN US, SO THAT HIS IMAGE IS SEEN MORE CLEARLY.

And the greatest work is love. Love is central to God's character. Throughout Scripture, love is shown to be our primary calling as His people. *"Love God"* and *"love your neighbour as yourself"* sum up the law and the prophets. Love is the last lesson Jesus teaches His disciples – in what He commands them at the Last Supper in John 15, and in what He shows them in His wonderful, remarkable sacrifice on the cross. Two thousand years ago, the invisible God made Himself plain for all to see in Jesus. Today, He wants to do the same again – this time, through us. And it's as we learn to receive God's love and give it wholeheartedly to others that the awesome, loving God of creation truly becomes visible.

TIME TO ACT

1   Take some time to reflect on these words from Genesis 1:27:

God created humankind in His own image.

Let the words *'in His own image'* wash over you. What does it mean to you to be made in God's image? Write down some words or draw a picture in response.

2   It's not just 'me' who is made in God's image. Every one of us is made by God – precious to Him and bearing His likeness. How does this impact the way you see your neighbours? Your colleagues? The people in your community? How can you help them to see God through your loving words and actions?

TIME TO PRAY

O God, my God –
I praise You because You've known me and loved me from the very beginning.

I give myself to You now. Help me to live in the light of Your love.

Make me into what You always planned for me to be – for Your glory.

Amen.

ONLY GOT A MINUTE?

- God created us and made us *"in His image"*.

- Every one of us is made by God and we are precious to Him.

- We model the likeness of Christ.

- As we become more like God, as we receive His love and give it wholeheartedly to others, the awesome, loving God of creation truly becomes visible.

Romans 1:20 (LWC)

I look at Your world. It shows me You're awesome and loving.

WOW! The world is AMAZING!

It is, Hal. But there's something even more amazing than this world. The awesome God who made it!

Our world is amazing. There's so much to make you say WOW! Big, blue skies. Giant, green trees. Bright, colourful flowers. Enormous elephants and tiny ants. Whales and dolphins, eagles and penguins – and so much more. And that's just on Earth! Look up into the sky at night and you'll see a million stars shining bright.

The Bible says that God made this wonderful world. It is His amazing artwork. Mountains, oceans, stars, fish, birds and animals – they all came from His BIG imagination. And He knows and cares for everything He made – including us. So next time you see something that makes you say WOW, turn it into worship. What a beautiful world. **And what an AWESOME God!**

TALK TOGETHER

Talk about all you've learnt about God's beautiful world together. What are your favourite animals, birds or fish? Why do you like them so much? Are there any places you love to visit – like the seaside or the woods? What do you love about them?

MAKE TOGETHER

God has made a beautiful world! Make some 'creation' biscuits. Cut them out using different shapes from creation – animal shapes, stars, flowers or people! As you bake, thank God for everything He has made.

PRAY TOGETHER

WOW, GOD! You are AMAZING! Thank you for the beautiful world that You made. Thank you that You love and care for everything in it – including me. I love You, God! **Amen.**

Beautiful World

TIME TO REFLECT

Romans 1:20

For since the creation of the world God's invisible qualities – his eternal power and divine nature – have been clearly seen, being understood from what has been made, so that people are without excuse.

Our world is incredible. And it points us towards God. The Bible says that there's something about exploring creation that helps us to grasp God Himself. It shows us God's 'eternal power'. Certainly, when we look at the mountains and the oceans, we get a sense of the limitless might of the God who made them. When we gaze up into the starry skies, we're overwhelmed by the size and the majesty of the God who put them in their place. And creation shows us God's 'divine nature'. Whether it's the delicate ecosystems – plants and living creatures working together and depending on each other to sustain life – or simply the irrepressible vegetation that returns year on year, nature testifies to a generous, caring God who fills the world with good things and provides for all He has made.

CREATION ITSELF IS A MIRACLE. AND THE MORE WE DISCOVER, THE MORE WONDERFUL IT SEEMS.

But this naturally begs the question: how often do we open ourselves up to experience its wonder? Every now and again we might be struck by the sight of a sunset, or by the star-speckled Universe surrounding us. But the rest of the time we're often too busy or distracted or disconnected to really appreciate the amazing world around us. There's a strong case, however, for making wonder in creation part of our lives – ultimately because it helps us to see the God it reveals and leads us to worship Him. And so, as we journey through this beautiful world, may we learn each day to see more of the might, the majesty, the benevolence and – above all – the incredible love of its awesome Creator.

TIME TO ACT

1 As you go through the day, make a conscious decision to find wonder in God's world. See all that God has given you – for example, the natural world around you, the food you have to eat, etc. Remember to say thank you!

2 Look over the list of ways to find wonder as a family on **page 65.** Select one that you could do this week to help build 'wonder worship' into your family life.

TIME TO PRAY

God of creation,
I praise You for the extraordinary
and beautiful world You have made.

How great You are, Lord.

Amen.

ONLY GOT A MINUTE?

- Our world is incredible. It points us towards God, showing us God's 'eternal power' and His limitless might.

- The more we discover, the more wonderful we realise God is.

- How often do we open ourselves up to experience the wonder of creation around us?

- Pause and make space to stop and wonder.

- How can you bring 'wonder worship' into your family life?

Beautiful World

Crafts and recipes

DEVOTION 5   BIRD FEEDER/FAT BALL

For a bird feeder:

- Pipe cleaner
- Cereal hoops
- Ribbon

1   Thread cereal hoops onto a pipe cleaner.

2   Mould the pipe cleaner into a circle shape and tie together.

3   Finish with a ribbon and hang up for the birds to enjoy.

For a fat ball pine cone:

- Pine cone
- Ribbon
- Seed-based bird food
- Peanut butter or lard

1   Tie a ribbon around the top of the pine cone so you can hang it on a branch.

2   Squish peanut butter or lard into the pine cone using your hands.

3   Roll the pine cone in bird seed.

4   Make sure it is really full so that the birds have lots of yummy food!

5   Hang up in your garden or a local park.

DEVOTION 1

DEVOTION 2

DEVOTION 3

Blow painting: light pictures

Mountain range collage

3D daffodils

DEVOTION 8   CREATION BISCUITS

You will need:
- 100g (4oz) Cheddar or other hard cheese, grated
- 400g (16oz) plain flour
- ½ tsp baking powder
- Salt and freshly ground black pepper, to taste
- 100g (4oz) butter, softened

1 Preheat oven to 200°C/180°C fan/gas mark 6 and grease a baking sheet or line with greaseproof paper.
2 Combine grated cheese, flour, baking powder, salt and pepper in a bowl.
3 Mix in butter and lightly knead into a dough either by hand or with an electric mixer.
4 Roll the dough out with a rolling pin so it is about 1cm thick.
5 Cut biscuits out into different animal and creation shapes and put on the baking sheet.
6 Put in the oven to cook for 10-12 minutes until golden.

DEVOTION 4

Cardboard star mobile

DEVOTION 6

Caterpillar paper chain

DEVOTION 7

Peg dolls

Beautiful World

Beautiful World

thank you prayers

Thank you, God, for Your whole world.

Thank you for windy rivers.

Thank you for tall mountains.

Thank you for green trees.

Thank you for blue seas.

Thank you for beautiful flowers.

Thank you for all the creatures.

Thank you for starry nights.

Thank you for my family... and me!

Thank you, God, that You have
the whole world in Your hands.

Amen.

Praise Party

Praise God with happy songs

Psalm 96:1 (LWC)

Sing to the Lord a **new song;** everybody sing to the Lord!

Wow! God is so amazing! And His love is so BIG! It makes me want to jump and cheer!

Go ahead! God loves it when we sing and dance to Him!

Think about the best news you ever heard. How does it make you feel? What does it make you do? It's hard to stay quiet. You want to cheer and sing as loudly as you can. And you can't keep still. Happy news makes us want to clap our hands and jump around!

The best news of all is that God made us, loves us and is always with us. That's why the Bible is packed full of people praising God. When they see how brilliant He is, they burst into song! And people are still singing today. All over the world, people are praising God for His amazing love. God loves to hear our praises. **So let's all sing and cheer and jump and dance to God!**

DEVOTION 1 EVERY MOVE I MAKE

TALK
TOGETHER

We praise God because He's amazing! Talk about all the things God has done for you and your family. What words describe God? Say thank you to Him!

MAKE
TOGETHER

We can join with Christians all over the world in praising God. Ask a grown-up to make a 'heart' stamp out of a potato or something similar. Draw a picture of yourself and the place where you live. Stamp hearts all over your picture, to remind yourself that God loves you and that we can love Him too.

PRAY
TOGETHER

Dear God, **thank you for my loud voice to sing to You.** Thank you for my bouncy legs to dance to You. Thank you that You are so amazing, so kind and so loving. **Amen.**

Praise Party

TIME TO REFLECT

Psalm 96

Sing to the Lord a new song; sing to the Lord, all the earth.
Sing to the Lord, praise his name; proclaim his salvation day after day.
Declare his glory among the nations, his marvelous deeds among all peoples.
For great is the Lord and most worthy of praise; he is to be feared above all gods.
For all the gods of the nations are idols, but the Lord made the heavens.
Splendour and majesty are before him; strength and glory are in his sanctuary.
Ascribe to the Lord, all you families of nations, ascribe to the Lord glory and strength.
Ascribe to the Lord the glory due his name; bring an offering and come into his courts.
Worship the Lord in the splendor of his holiness; tremble before him, all the earth.
Say among the nations, "The Lord reigns."
The world is firmly established, it cannot be moved; he will judge the peoples with equity.
Let the heavens rejoice, let the earth be glad; let the sea resound, and all that is in it.
Let the fields be jubilant, and everything in them; let all the trees of the forest sing for joy.
Let all creation rejoice before the Lord, for he comes, he comes to judge the earth.
He will judge the world in righteousness and the peoples in his faithfulness.

Praise is the soundtrack to Scripture. In the Old Testament, God's people sing epic songs of praise to celebrate God's victory and might. Songs burst from the pages of Israel's great hymn book, the Psalms. Praise flows from individual men and women of faith after life-changing encounters with God – as in Hannah's prayer after God grants her a child (1 Samuel 2), or Mary's song in Luke 1. Doxologies, hymns sung by the early Christians, are scattered throughout Paul's letters to the early church. Some of the simplest and most memorable exclamations of praise are those said by the angels, such as the one the shepherds heard (Luke 2) or those said at the throne of God Himself (Revelation 4).

Why does praise feature so heavily in the Bible? Ultimately, because God deserves it.

As the psalmist writes, *"Great is the Lord and most worthy of praise"* (verse 4).

AND AS WE SEEK TO FOLLOW GOD, PRAISE SHOULD BE A KEY FEATURE IN OUR LIVES TOO.

It's part and parcel of knowing Him. The more we see of God, His majesty and His goodness, the more we want to praise Him. But praise also gets the dynamic of our relationship right. We live in a highly 'individualistic' culture – one that puts 'me' and 'my needs' first. But when we come to God in praise, we put ourselves, our desires and even our concerns to one side, to give God that which is His due. We lay down who we are to declare all that God is – and to celebrate all that God has done and continues to do, in the world and in our lives.

TIME TO ACT

1   Praising God includes telling Him how great He is, thanking Him for all He has done and expressing our love for Him. Take some time now to sing or speak praise to God. You might want to use a psalm from the Bible, such as Psalm 96, or you could use more modern worship songs.

2   In 1 Chronicles 16, where Psalm 96 is originally found, David calls the Levites to lead the people into praise. Sometimes, we need to be the ones to lead our family into a place of thanksgiving and praise. Think about ways you might make praise and thanksgiving common features of your day-to-day family life.

TIME TO PRAY

I praise You, God, for all that You are – my Maker, Provider, Healer and Saviour.

I praise You, God, for all that You have done and all that You continue to do.

May You find a song of praise on my lips, now and always.

Amen.

ONLY GOT A MINUTE?

- Encounters with God lead to praise.

- Praising God changes the dynamic of our relationship with Him.

- When we come to God in praise, we put ourselves, our desires and our concerns to one side.

- Choosing to praise God recentres us, allowing us to truly celebrate all that He has done and continues to do, in the world and in our lives.

- How might you make praise and thanksgiving important in your day-to-day family life?

Praise Party

Praise God with your soul and strength

Luke 10:27

Love the Lord your God with all your **heart**, with all your **soul**, with all your **mind** and with all your **strength**.

I feel like my heart is full of love for God!

That's great, Hal! The more you love God, the more you want to praise Him and make Him happy.

Can you find your hand? What about your foot? Your nose? Your knees? Well done! Can you find your heart? What about your mind? Your soul? It's not so easy to find these. But they are very important. They're the bits inside of us which choose what we think, say and do. And we can praise God with them too!

Loving God with heart, soul, mind and strength means making God the most important person in our lives. It means loving Him best, putting Him first, and giving Him our all. **It's not always easy to love somebody we can't see.** But we can get to know God and the things He loves by reading about Him in the Bible.

TALK TOGETHER

Talk about all the different ways you show people that you love them. How can you show God that you love Him? **What makes God happy?**

MAKE TOGETHER

We can love God with every part of our body. We can praise him with our breath. Make some paper windmills, which turn when you blow hard. You can't see the wind that pushes them but you can see the result. Just like the wind, we can't see God, but we can see the marvellous things he has done.

PRAY TOGETHER

Dear God, **thank you that You love me more than I can imagine.** Help me to love You too, with every part of me. **Amen.**

Praise Party

2 TIME TO REFLECT

Luke 10:25-28

On one occasion an expert in the law stood up to test Jesus.
"Teacher," he asked, "what must I do to inherit eternal life?"
"What is written in the Law?" he replied. "How do you read it?"
He answered, "'Love the Lord your God with all your heart and with all your soul
and with all your strength and with all your mind'; and, 'Love your neighbour as yourself.'"
"You have answered correctly," Jesus replied. "Do this and you will live."

It's often said that we only see the tip of an iceberg. Dive underneath the surface and you'll discover a whole mountain of ice below. The same is true of our praise. What we say or sing isn't the sum of our praise. Rather, it's an outward expression of something bigger and deeper within us: our love for God.

TRUE PRAISE BEGINS IN THE HEART.

It flows from a commitment to the ancient command, reiterated by Jesus Himself, to love God with all our heart, soul, mind and strength. The Bible asks us to orientate every part of our lives towards God – our words, actions, thoughts and dreams – all for Him and His glory. Anything less is merely paying lip-service to Him.

Real worship, then, involves giving every part of ourselves to God. And yet, far from losing out, we find we're left with more than we started with. When Jesus says, *"Do this and you will live"*, he isn't talking about gaining brownie points with God or earning a ticket into heaven. There's a sense here that giving our all to God is what makes us really come alive. Again, this command – to love God and love our neighbour as ourselves – is at odds with modern Western culture. It places 'me', my dreams and my desires some way down the pecking order. But the Bible promises that the more we give, the more we will receive (Luke 6:38). When we place all that we are and all that we have in God's hands, we discover that God will do more in us and through us than we could ever ask or imagine.

TIME TO ACT

1   Take some time to reflect on what it means to love God with heart, soul, mind and strength. You might like to ask yourself:

- **Heart:** What or who is your number one priority?

- **Soul:** What do you strive after? What are you ambitious for?

- **Mind:** What or whom do you spend most of your time thinking about?

- **Strength:** What do you use most of your time, money and energy for?

2   Read Deuteronomy 6:4-9, where this teaching first appears. It instructs parents to impress God's commands on their children and embed them into family life. How might you learn to love God and follow His commands as a family? Can you think of any opportunities to serve God together?

TIME TO PRAY

Thank you, Father, that You love me.

I'm sorry for the times when I fail to love You as I should.

Help me to give You the very best of me – heart, soul, mind and strength.

Amen.

60 SECONDS

ONLY GOT A MINUTE?

- True praise flows from a commitment to love God, with all our heart, soul, mind and strength.

- Real worship involves giving every part of us to God.

- When we place all that we are and all that we have in God's hands, we discover that He will do more in us, and through us, than we could ever ask or imagine.

- What do you strive after? What are you ambitious for? What are God's ambitions for you?

BIG

Praise Party

Based on Psalm 150:3-5 (LWC)

Praise God –
He is so great!
Praise Him with the loud
trumpet. Praise Him with
guitars and violins.
Praise Him with drums
and whistles. Praise Him
with tambourines and
maracas!

Wow! A big drum! Can I use this to praise God?

Of course! God loves it when we make music to Him!

Do you have any musical instruments? There are so many to choose from! Some you hit – like big loud drums. Some you shake – like jingling bells and tambourines. Some you blow – like trumpets, recorders and kazoos. Some you strum – like guitars. And on a keyboard, you let your fingers go for a LONG run!

We can use all of these to praise God. People have been making music to God for thousands of years. In Bible times, people used horns, cymbals and harps to make big, beautiful sounds to God. Sometimes music can show our feelings better that words can. We might not know how to tell God we love Him. **But we can make a happy noise to Him to show Him!**

TALK
TOGETHER

How many instruments can you name? What sounds do they make? Which do you like best? Think about how God loves to hear praise music – because He loves the people who play it to Him!

MAKE
TOGETHER

We can praise God by making music to Him. Why don't you have a go at making your own instruments? Try filling empty jam jars with different amounts of water and then tap them with a metal teaspoon. Lots of water makes low deep notes and a little water makes high notes. You can also bang big saucepans with a wooden spoon to make a drum, or make shakers by filling empty plastic bottles with a handful of dried rice or pasta. Make sure you screw the lid on tight!

PRAY
TOGETHER

Dear God, thank you for beautiful music. Thank you for all the different sounds I can make for You. Help me to praise You wherever I am and whatever I'm doing. Amen.

TIME TO REFLECT

Psalm 150

Praise the Lord.

Praise God in his sanctuary; praise him in his mighty heavens.

Praise him for his acts of power; praise him for his surpassing greatness.

Praise him with the sounding of the trumpet, praise him with the harp and lyre,
praise him with tambourine and dancing, praise him with the strings and pipe,
praise him with the clash of cymbals, praise him with resounding cymbals.

Let everything that has breath praise the Lord.

Praise the Lord.

The Book of Psalms is arguably the finest worship book in history. And this final psalm is one last rallying cry to praise God. In many ways it sums up the whole subject – a kind of 'blueprint' for community praise. In just six verses, it outlines where we should praise (verse 1), why we should praise (verse 2), how we should praise (verses 3-5) and who is invited to praise God (verse 6). To anybody used to going to church regularly, this will all look and sound familiar. The psalmist calls people to the 'sanctuary' – that is, somewhere holy and set apart, for praise purposes – where they're called to make music, sing and dance in celebration of all that God is and all that He's done.

But this psalm does more than just offer a template for worship. It reminds us how wonderful it is to praise God together – that it is *good* to make a big noise in His honour. It sounds obvious, but it's something that, in our digital age, we can sometimes forget. The internet has given us a host of worship and teaching resources at our fingertips, as well as access to online faith forums. It would be very easy for praise to become something we offer quietly and privately. But there's a dynamic that comes from worshipping together that pleases God and increases our own faith. What's more, it provides an important witness within our communities.

GOD'S HEART IS THAT ALL COME TO KNOW AND PRAISE HIM.

Our worship points others towards the One that it's for. And the louder the praise, the more people will hear it.

TIME TO ACT

1   Psalm 150 says:

Praise him for his acts of power,
Praise him for his magnificent greatness.

Psalm 150:2 (The Message)

Say, write or draw what this means to you.

2   We sometimes think of our Christian life as a solo run. But it's more like a marathon event, with thousands of people running together and cheering each other on. Take some time to pray for your church family. Pray for the leaders as they seek to serve God and your community. Pray for all those who are involved in leading or supporting the children's ministry.

TIME TO PRAY

Thank you, God, that we can praise You.

Thank you that we are invited to be part of your big story for all of creation.

Help us to declare Your goodness loudly enough for all to hear.

Amen.

60 SECONDS

ONLY GOT A MINUTE?

- The Bible is full of stories of people joining together to worship God.

- Joining with others to worship together pleases God and increases our own faith.

- Sometimes we can think of our Christian life as a solo run. But it's more like a marathon event, with thousands of people running together and cheering each other on.

- Pray for your church family and for those who encourage you in your faith. How can you be an 'encourager' to those around you?

BIG

Praise Party

Be still and **know** that I am **God.**

Psalm 46:10

Praise in the Psalms
A TEN-MINUTE MEDITATION

You will need a quiet space, a Bible, a notebook and a pen.

- **Find a quiet space.** Sit down and make yourself comfortable. Breathe slowly and deeply. Become aware of God's presence with you and thank Him.

- **Choose a psalm to read** – for example, Psalm 23. Invite God's Spirit to speak to you as you read.

- **Slowly read through the psalm once.**
  Slowly read through the psalm again.
  Look back over the psalm.
  Was there a particular verse that stood out to you?

- **Meditate on the verse** by emphasising each word in turn.
  For example, verse 6:

  > ***Surely*** *your goodness and love will follow me all the days of my life...*
  >
  > *Surely **your** goodness and love will follow me all the days of my life...*
  >
  > *Surely your **goodness** and love will follow me all the days of my life...*

- **What is God revealing to you** as you reflect on these words?
  How is He encouraging you?
  How is He challenging you?

- **Use these reflections** as you pray and praise.

- **If you have time...**
  Rewrite the psalm or a section of the psalm in your own words.
  Alternatively, draw a picture based on your reflections.
  Use it as a means of praising God.

Praise Party

Ephesians 5:1 (LWC)

See what God does, and then go and do it yourself!

I love God! I want to go where He goes. I want to do what He does...

You can, Hal. Just look at Jesus. He'll show you how.

Have you got a best friend? What are they like? When we make friends, we get to know them. We find out what makes them happy and what they like to do. And we have *lots* of fun doing those things together!

It's a bit like this with God. One big reason to praise God is because He's our friend. And being friends with God means getting to know Him and learning to follow Him. We can do this by looking at Jesus. **The Bible says that God sent his Son, Jesus, to live with us.** We can see what's special to God – what He cares about – by seeing all that Jesus did. And nothing makes God happier than when we learn to do those things too.

TALK
TOGETHER

Look at the stories of Jesus in the gospels. What kinds of things did Jesus do? What does it say about what God is like – what He cares about? How can we do likewise?

MAKE
TOGETHER

We can praise God by following in Jesus' footsteps. Do some feet-painting pictures… As you do them, think about how learning about Jesus and doing what He did makes God really happy!

PRAY
TOGETHER

Dear God, **thank you that You are my best friend.** Thank you for sending Jesus to show me what You are like. Help me to follow in Your footsteps every day. **Amen.**

Praise Party

TIME TO REFLECT

Ephesians 5:1-2 (The Message)

Watch what God does, and then you do it, like children who learn proper behaviour from their parents. Mostly what God does is love you. Keep company with him and learn a life of love. Observe how Christ loved us. His love was not cautious but extravagant. He didn't love in order to get something from us but to give everything of himself to us. Love like that.

"Praise the LORD, my soul, and forget not all his benefits – who forgives all your sins and heals all your diseases…" (Psalm 103:2-3). God's goodness is a recurring theme throughout the Psalms. They paint a picture of a God who loves passionately and cares tenderly. And this portrait gains a new dimension in Jesus. For in Jesus, the invisible God became visible. "No one has ever seen God," John wrote, "but the one and only Son… has made him known" (John 1:18). Jesus lives all that the Psalms declare. He heals the sick. He welcomes the lonely. He lifts up the humble. He binds up the broken-hearted. The more we see of Jesus, the more we begin to grasp just how deep the Father's love runs. And our response is surely one of wonder and worship.

But this is only half the story. 'Watch what God does, and then you do it,' Paul tells the Ephesians. "Observe how Christ loved us… Love like that." It's God's desire that we become like Him, "walking in the way of love" (verse 2, NIV). But rather than give us a textbook, He gives us Jesus. As we spend time with Him, we see what matters to God. How His love is not just for 'me', but for my neighbour. And for the poor and marginalised – those at the edges of our communities. The more we're with Him, the more we'll become like Him – following in His footsteps and offering hope in all we say and do. In Jesus, God invites us to experience His immense love for us.

AS WE "KEEP COMPANY" WITH HIM, LET'S PRAY THAT IT'S NOT JUST OUR HEARTS THAT ARE MOVED IN PRAISE, BUT OUR FEET TOO.

TIME TO ACT

1   Paul writes that we should "keep company" with God. Jesus shows us the importance of finding rest and refreshment with the Father, regularly retreating from the hustle and bustle of a busy life to spend time with God. Find some time today to rest in God's presence – whether that's with music, the Bible or simply silence. You might like to try our ten-minute meditation, found on **page 107**.

2   As we look at Jesus, we don't just discover how God loves us, but how we are to love in turn. Who would Jesus be spending time with in your community and friendship circle? Where might God be calling you to follow Him? Pray for God's strength to go where He's leading you.

TIME TO PRAY

Thank you, God,
that we love because You first loved us.

Help me to see more of You.

Help me to be more like You.

Lead me in a life of love,
walking with You each step of the way.

Amen.

ONLY GOT A MINUTE?

- The Psalms describe a God who loves us passionately and cares for us tenderly.

- In Jesus, this invisible God becomes visible.

- The more we see of Jesus, the more we begin to grasp how much God loves us.

- Through Jesus, God invites us to experience His immense love for us. As we **"keep company"** with Him, let not just our hearts be moved in praise, but our feet too, as we share His love with those around us.

- Find a moment to **"keep company"** with God today.

Praise Party

Psalm 136:1 (LWC)

Say a great big thank you to God! He is so good to us! His love never, ever runs out!

Animals are amazing! Ice cream is amazing! GOD'S LOVE is amazing!

They're all gifts from God, Hal. Is there something you want to say to Him?

Some words are really special. And there are two words that make people really happy when we say them. We might say them after we get a present. Or when somebody gives us a tasty meal. Or when someone helps us with something that's a bit tricky. Do you know what they are? That's right – THANK YOU!

The Bible says that we can praise God by saying "thank you" to Him. He has done so much for us. He made a wonderful world that we can enjoy. He gives us all we need, like clothes and food and family. And best of all, He gave us Jesus. Because of Jesus, we can be friends with God forever. **And that's worth the biggest THANK YOU of them all!**

TALK TOGETHER

There's so much to thank God for! Can you think of five things to say thank you for today? You might want to draw them on sticky notes and put them up around the house, so you never forget to thank God!

MAKE TOGETHER

Nothing will ever stop us from being God's friend. Create a 'thankfulness peacock' using a paper plate, coloured card and paint. Cut a skittle-shaped head and body out of the coloured card and stick it onto the plate. Draw or stick two eyes and a beak onto the card. Make incisions in the paper plate towards the body to create feathers. On each feather, write something to be thankful for. Decorate your peacock with paint and glitter.

PRAY TOGETHER

Dear God, thank you for all that You give to me. Thank you for food and clothes, for friends and family. Thank you that You sent Jesus so that I can always be Your friend. Amen.

Praise Party

TIME TO REFLECT

Psalm 136

Give thanks to the Lord, for he is good.	*His love endures for ever.*
Give thanks to the God of gods.	*His love endures for ever.*
Give thanks to the Lord of lords:	*His love endures for ever.*
to him who alone does great wonders,	*His love endures for ever.*
who by his understanding made the heavens,	*His love endures for ever.*
who spread out the earth upon the waters,	*His love endures for ever.*
who made the great lights –	*His love endures for ever.*
the sun to govern the day,	*His love endures for ever.*
the moon and stars to govern the night;	*His love endures for ever.*
to him who struck down the firstborn of Egypt	*His love endures for ever.*
and brought Israel out from among them	*His love endures for ever.*
with a mighty hand and outstretched arm;	*His love endures for ever.*
to him who divided the Red Sea asunder	*His love endures for ever.*
and brought Israel through the midst of it,	*His love endures for ever.*
but swept Pharaoh and his army into the Red Sea;	*His love endures for ever.*
to him who led his people through the wilderness;	*His love endures for ever.*
to him who struck down great kings,	*His love endures for ever.*
and killed mighty kings –	*His love endures for ever.*
Sihon king of the Amorites	*His love endures for ever.*
and Og king of Bashan –	*His love endures for ever.*
and gave their land as an inheritance,	*His love endures for ever.*
an inheritance to his servant Israel.	*His love endures for ever.*
He remembered us in our low estate	*His love endures for ever.*
and freed us from our enemies.	*His love endures for ever.*
He gives food to every creature.	*His love endures for ever.*
Give thanks to the God of heaven.	*His love endures for ever.*

Thanksgiving and praise are two sides of the same coin – so much so that if you look in the dictionary, you'll find 'praise' defined as 'expressing gratitude'. In Old Testament times, songs of praise were sung whilst thank-offerings were made in the temple – the two together a fitting celebration of God's victory and rescue. It's likely that Psalm 136 was used in this way. In this psalm, the leader calls on the congregation to thank God for all the marvellous things He has done. And there is so much to celebrate. God is not only an awesome Creator and Provider. He is also their wonderful Saviour. He freed them from slavery in Egypt and gave them an amazing inheritance – the

Promised Land. This is their story; this is their song – the reason for a thousand thanksgivings.

AND THIS IS OUR SONG TOO. GOD, OUR CREATOR AND PROVIDER, IS ALSO OUR SAVIOUR.

In Jesus, we have been rescued. We've been set free from the power of sin: now there's nothing to keep us from God's love. And we've been given a new inheritance. God calls us His children: we can know His presence, peace and power, today and forever more. This isn't just a nice theological idea. It's a story that changes our present reality and our future hope. Having been given such an incredible gift, saying thank you is just the beginning. In temple worship, praise was accompanied by an offering. As we celebrate all that God has done for us, we, too, are called to make an offering... in the words of the old hymn, nothing less than *"my soul, my life, my all"* (Isaac Watts).

TIME TO ACT

1   Write your own version of Psalm 136. List all the things God has done for you – the times when He has shown His love and faithfulness in your life. Add the refrain *"His love endures forever"* after each line.

2   We don't always find time to say thank you. We may need some help to make a habit of gratitude. Why not try setting an alarm on your phone for every couple of hours? When it pings, think of five things to thank God for – and thank Him!

TIME TO PRAY

Father God – You have given everything *to* me. You have given everything *for* me. Accept my thanks. Accept my praise. Accept my life, laid down to live for You.

Amen.

ONLY GOT A MINUTE?

- Psalm 136 reminds the congregation of God's enduring love, throughout their history.

- God intervened again and again to change their present reality and to give them a future hope.

- That same God is also our Saviour.

- In Jesus, we have been rescued. We've been set free from the power of sin, so now there's nothing to keep us from God's love.

- How can you create a habit of gratitude? Try setting an alarm on your phone each day. When it pings, think of five things to thank God for – and thank Him!

Praise Party

Romans 12:10-13 (LWC)

Always **love** one another. Be **joyful** and **faithful** and patient. **Share** with people in need. Practise being **kind**.

Wow! God's love is SO BIG! I can't keep it to myself!

Well, Hal, why don't you share it with someone? That makes God really happy!

There are lots of ways to let people know you love them. Telling them is one way. But we can show them too. Doing kind and helpful things shows people how much we care for them and it makes them happy.

It's the same with praising God. We can praise Him with songs and prayers. But we can also show Him how much we love Him by the things we do. In the Bible, God asks us to share His love with the people around us. Every time we help people in need, we make God happy. Every time we do kind things for others, we make God happy. And when we do all these things, **we show other people how much God loves them too!**

TALK TOGETHER

Think about how you could show God's love to those around you this week. What kind things could you do for the people in your street? Are there any people in your community who might need your help?

MAKE TOGETHER

We can praise God by loving other people. Bake some 'love bug' biscuits. Why not share them with your friends and neighbours?

PRAY TOGETHER

Dear God, **thank you that Your love for me is really BIG!** Help me to share Your love with other people so that they can see how much You love them too. **Amen.**

6 TIME TO REFLECT

Romans 12:9-18

Love must be sincere. Hate what is evil; cling to what is good. Be devoted to one another in love. Honour one another above yourselves. Never be lacking in zeal, but keep your spiritual fervour, serving the Lord. Be joyful in hope, patient in affliction, faithful in prayer. Share with the Lord's people who are in need. Practise hospitality.

Bless those who persecute you; bless and do not curse. Rejoice with those who rejoice; mourn with those who mourn. Live in harmony with one another. Do not be proud, but be willing to associate with people of low position. Do not be conceited.

Do not repay anyone evil for evil. Be careful to do what is right in the eyes of everyone. If it is possible, as far as it depends on you, live at peace with everyone.

When we think about 'praising God', it's probably the things we say or sing which spring to mind. But praise is also expressed in the things we do. Word and deed go hand in hand, because the things we do make good on the things we say. It's a connection that Jesus Himself makes to His disciples at the Last Supper: *"If you love me,"* He tells them, *"keep my commands."* (John 14:15). Praise is not just a matter of our mouths, then, but of our hearts and hands too. We can tell God how wonderful He is. We can acknowledge all He has done. We can really and truly feel the deepest gratitude for everything He has given to us. But the next step is to take our love for God and channel it into love for our neighbour.

Paul's words to the Romans show us what this looks like in practice.

AS CHRISTIANS, OUR LIVES ARE TO BE CHARACTERISED BY HUMILITY, GENEROSITY, SERVICE AND SACRIFICE.

We're called to be pastors (guiding and supporting others) and peacemakers. These are undoubtedly challenging commands to take on board. We naturally strive to do the best for our family. But what about our neighbours or our children's friends? Can we love them as we love ourselves? Paul asks that we practise hospitality. Are we willing to see our homes as God-given resources at His disposal? Are we prepared to disrupt our precious family traditions to show God's love to those who really need to see it? True obedience is hard – but God is worth it. As we learn to praise Him, may we always pray that our actions speak even louder than our words.

TIME TO ACT

1 Generosity flows from a thankful heart. Make a list of all the material resources you have. Pray over them with thanksgiving. How might God be asking you to use them – with your family and friends, your community, or further afield?

2 The Book of Amos underscores the importance of connecting words and deeds in our worship. In it, the people of God come under serious criticism for saying all the right things to God in the temple, whilst exploiting the poor in their day-to-day lives. In Amos 5:21-24, God emphatically rejects their songs and sacrifices, calling for justice and righteousness instead.

Amos reminds us again that love for God is expressed in love for neighbour – especially the vulnerable and oppressed. Spend some time researching organisations that are working to help those in crisis – for example, anti-slavery groups or homeless charities. How might you partner with them, in prayer or financially?

TIME TO PRAY

Father God – help me to love those around me, when it's easy and when it's difficult.

Please accept everything I am and everything I have as an offering of praise.

Amen.

ONLY GOT A MINUTE?

- Praise isn't just expressed through our mouths; praise is also expressed in the things we do.

- An overflowing of praise results in an outpouring of love for those around us – our family, our neighbours, our community and our world.

- Generosity flows from a thankful heart. Thank God for all the material resources you have. How might God be asking you to use them as an offering of praise and thanksgiving?

- Who is your neighbour?

For the LORD
is **good** and His love
endures forever;
His **faithfulness** continues
through **all generations.**

Psalm
100:5

A psalm for all seasons

PRAYING AND PRAISING THROUGH THE PSALMS

Psalm 100

When you feel joyful –
or need to remind yourself of God's goodness...

... Enter His gates with thanksgiving and His courts with praise;
give thanks to Him and praise His name.
For the LORD is good and His love endures forever;
His faithfulness continues through all generations.

Psalm 23

When you feel blessed – or need to know that God cares...

The LORD is my shepherd, I lack nothing.
He makes me lie down in green pastures,
He leads me beside quiet waters, He refreshes my soul...

Psalm 46

When you feel anxious or afraid...

God is our refuge and strength, an ever-present help in trouble.
Therefore we will not fear, though the earth give way
and the mountains fall into the heart of the sea...

Psalm 25

When you feel like quitting...

Guard my life and rescue me;
do not let me be put to shame, for I take refuge in you.
May integrity and uprightness protect me,
because my hope, LORD, is in you.

Psalm 8

When you feel amazed by God's love –
or need to be reminded of how precious you are to Him...

When I consider your heavens, the work of your fingers,
the moon and the stars, which you have set in place,
what is mankind that you are mindful of them,
human beings that you care for them?

Praise Party

Ecclesiastes 3 (LWC)

There is a time for **everything.**
A time to **play,**
a time to **sleep,**
a time to **read,**
a time to **bounce,**
a time to **eat** and
a time to **party!**

Is it time for the praise party yet?

Yes, Hal. Get yourself ready – it's time to party!

Have you ever been to a party? What was it for? What did you do there? A party is a celebration. 'Celebrate' means being happy and having fun because of something or someone really special. We don't have parties every day. But it's important that we have them, because some things are worth celebrating!

There are lots of ways to praise God. We can tell God that we love Him quietly, when we're by ourselves. But God loves it when we throw Him a praise party! When we go to church, we meet up with our friends and celebrate God's great big love together. And the party's not just for us to enjoy. We can invite everyone we know to come and praise God too!

TALK TOGETHER

Talk about going to church. How is it like a party in God's honour? What other things do we do at church that make God happy? (For example: learning about Jesus.)

MAKE TOGETHER

God's love for us deserves the biggest party in the world! Make paper chains out of strips of bright, coloured paper. Or stick coloured triangles to a long piece of string to make bunting. Write things to be thankful for on your paper chains/bunting. Put them up and have a praise party with your family and friends!

PRAY TOGETHER

Dear God, **thank you for praise parties!** Thank you for special times to jump and sing to You with my friends. Thank you, too, that every day with You is special, because You are my friend. **Amen.**

TIME TO REFLECT

Ecclesiastes 3:1-8

There is a time for everything, and a season for every activity under the heavens:
a time to be born and a time to die, a time to plant and a time to uproot,
a time to kill and a time to heal, a time to tear down and a time to build,
a time to weep and a time to laugh, a time to mourn and a time to dance,
a time to scatter stones and a time to gather them, a time to embrace
and a time to refrain from embracing,
a time to search and a time to give up, a time to keep and a time to throw away,
a time to tear and a time to mend, a time to be silent and a time to speak,
a time to love and a time to hate, a time for war and a time for peace.

Some days it's easy to praise God. Other days it's really hard. Sometimes we feel God's presence and blessings. At other times, God feels distant, prayers seem to go unanswered and struggles seem to swamp us like a landslide. At these times, the last thing we might want to do is praise God. That's why it's helpful to read passages like the third chapter of Ecclesiastes. It reminds us that our lives will inevitably pass through different seasons. There'll be times when things are going well, when it's easy to praise and thank God. But there'll also be times of challenge or heartache, when it may take more emotional effort and commitment to praise God. At these times it can feel like a sacrifice.

This is one reason why being part of a worshipping church community is so helpful. It provides a spiritual rhythm to our lives, ensuring there's regular time set aside each week to praise God – however we may be feeling. It's worth noting that praise in the Bible is often referred to in terms of 'sacrifice'.

SOMETIMES, AS AN EXHAUSTED PARENT, JUST TURNING UP AT CHURCH ON A SUNDAY IS A MAJOR ACT OF SACRIFICE AND THEREFORE AN ACT OF PRAISE!

But church also provides us with a spiritual momentum. We can be carried into a place of praise when we don't feel strong enough to get there by ourselves. Church is a family, sharing in life's ups and downs and helping each other through. Being with others who understand the joys and challenges we face is invaluable.

It's God's grace to us – to help us know Him in each season and keep us praising Him.

TIME TO ACT

1   In Philippians 4:4, Paul says that we should "rejoice in the Lord always". Take some time to reflect on what that means to you:

- **Rejoice** – Is this the same as feeling happy? Or does it have to do with thanking God for His promises to us, and trusting in Him?

- **In the Lord** – What are the things that God has given to us because of Jesus? What does that mean for us – in good times and in hard times?

- **Always** – Is there anything right now that is stopping you from praising God? Bring it to Him, confident that He is big enough to hold it – and you!

2   Think about people within your church community who may be going through a challenging time. Take time to commit them to God in prayer. Might God be asking you to provide practical support too?

TIME TO PRAY

Father God, thank you that whatever I go through, You are always with me.

Help me to keep praising You through the sunshine and the rain.

Amen.

60 SECONDS

ONLY GOT A MINUTE?

- In times of challenge or heartache it takes more emotional effort and commitment to praise God.

- Being part of a worshipping church community provides a spiritual rhythm to our lives.

- Being with others who understand the joys and challenges we face can help us to be carried into a place of praise when we don't feel strong enough to get there by ourselves.

- Is there anything right now that is stopping you from praising God? Bring it to Him and be confident that He is big enough to hold it – and you!

BIG

Praise Party

Psalm 146:2 (LWC)

I'm gonna **praise God** my whole life long! **I'll sing to God** for as long as I'm alive!

Oh, no! The praise party's nearly over!

Don't worry, Hal. The party might come to an end. But that doesn't mean you need to stop praising!

That's right. You can never run out of things to praise God for!

Do you have a favourite place you like to visit? Maybe it's your favourite park. Maybe it's your granny's house. Maybe it's somewhere far away, where you go for holidays. Our world is really BIG. It's bursting with exciting places to discover. And no matter how many places we've already been to, there's always more to see and explore!

It's like this with God. God is so BIG! His love is so big. And as we get bigger, we'll find there's much, much more to discover – about how amazing He is and how much He loves us. We've looked at some of the ways we can praise God. But that's just the beginning. **Learning to love and praise God is the adventure of a lifetime!**

TALK TOGETHER

Talk about all the different things you've learnt about praising God. Where can we praise God? How can we show Him that we love Him? What's been your favourite way of praising God?

MAKE TOGETHER

We can praise God all our life! Make a picture frame by getting a grown-up to cut out a rectangle on one side of an old cereal box. This makes your frame. Put stickers over the edge or paint your frame. Draw your favourite place to go inside.

PRAY TOGETHER

Dear God, **thank you that You are GREATER than I can imagine.** Thank you that Your love for me is BIGGER than I can imagine. Help me to keep on praising You my whole life long! **Amen.**

Praise Party

TIME TO REFLECT

Psalm 146

Praise the Lord. Praise the Lord, my soul.
I will praise the Lord all my life; I will sing praise to my God as long as I live.
Do not put your trust in princes, in human beings, who cannot save.
When their spirit departs, they return to the ground;
on that very day their plans come to nothing.
Blessed are those whose help is the God of Jacob, whose hope is in the Lord their God.
He is the Maker of heaven and earth, the sea, and everything in them –
he remains faithful forever.
He upholds the cause of the oppressed and gives food to the hungry.
The Lord sets prisoners free, the Lord gives sight to the blind,
the Lord lifts up those who are bowed down, the Lord loves the righteous.
The Lord watches over the foreigner and sustains the fatherless and the widow,
but he frustrates the ways of the wicked.
The Lord reigns forever, your God, O Zion, for all generations.
Praise the Lord.

Psalm 146 is a song about commitment. It opens with a vow – the psalmist pledging to praise God for as long as life endures, and to make worship a lifetime endeavour. The invitation is there for us to do the same. The Bible gives us insights into what this looks like in practice. It's praising God quietly, when it's just us and God. It's praising God loudly in the congregation, with the sound of many voices and instruments. It's whispering praise to God at the many wonders we see around us each day. It's celebrating the good things God has given us and sharing them with others. It's trusting God when things are tough. And it's giving our lives to His service, committing ourselves to go where He leads and do all He asks.

This kind of vow isn't for the faint-hearted. As promises go, it's a big one. But at the heart of this psalm lies a much bigger promise – God's promise to us. If there's one thing that jumps out from Psalm 146, it's God's faithfulness.

WE WORSHIP THE GOD OF ETERNITY — WHO WAS THERE AT THE BEGINNING AND WILL REIGN FOR GENERATIONS TO COME.

And this same, majestic God of the universe cares deeply for all He has made. He hears our cries. He watches over the weakest and champions their cause. He is on our side. With Him, we cannot lose. As we walk with God day by day, season by season, we will learn and relearn His faithful love for us. And as we do, our praise will resound, not just throughout our lives, but as an echo throughout eternity.

TIME TO ACT

1   Create a 'map' of your journey with God, from the time you first committed to Him until now. Where have you walked with Him? What have been the faith landmarks along the way – the points where you saw God's faithfulness first-hand? Use this to praise Him.

2   Reflect on ways in which you can praise God each day as a family. For example, you might create a praise wall in the house. At a regular time each day, write up answers to prayer, something to be thankful for or words of love for God, and stick them to the wall. Write your thoughts and prayers in a family praise book.

TIME TO PRAY

Father God –

Nothing I could say, nothing I could do, could ever thank you enough for Your wonderful love and faithfulness.

But still I pray:

"Take my life and let it be consecrated, Lord, to thee.
Take my moments and my days.
Let them flow in ceaseless praise."
(Frances Ridley Havergal)

Amen.

60 SECONDS

ONLY GOT A MINUTE?

- In Psalm 146, the psalmist pledges to praise God for as long as life endures, and to make worship a lifetime endeavour.

- We worship the God of eternity, who was there at the beginning and will reign for generations to come.

- This majestic, eternal God is forever for us. He is on our side. With Him, we cannot lose.

- What is your map of your journey with God? From the time you first committed to Him until now, where have you walked with Him? When have you seen God's faithfulness first-hand?

BIG

Crafts and recipes

DEVOTION 2   PAPER WINDMILL

You will need:

- Split pin
- Square of paper
- Straw
- Plasticine or sticky tack
- Pencil

1 Fold your square of paper in half to make two triangles, unfold and fold the other way. You will now have a piece of paper with two diagonal folds.

2 Let your child decorate both sides of the paper with crayons.

3 Cut along each of the diagonal lines, from the corners to two-thirds to the centre.

4 Fold the four corner sections down to the centre of the paper, holding each section under your thumb at the centre as you work.

5 Once all four triangles are in place, put a blob of plasticine on top. With a very sharp pencil, pierce through all the layers to make a hole that you can then thread a split pin through.

6 Open the split pin and grip it around the top of a straw. You will need to work your windmill around a few times to make sure it moves smoothly.

DEVOTION 1

Potato stamping

DEVOTION 3

Home-made musical instruments

DEVOTION 4

Feet painting

DEVOTION 6 — LOVE BUG BISCUITS

You will need:

- 200g (8oz) butter, softened
- 200g (8oz) sugar
- 1 large egg
- ½ tsp vanilla extract
- 400g (16oz) plain flour, plus extra for dusting
- Icing sugar
- Food colouring
- Edible eyes
- Rolling pin
- Heart-shaped cutter

1. Preheat oven to 200°C/180°C fan/gas mark 6 and grease or line a baking sheet.
2. Mix the butter and sugar by hand or with an electric mixer.
3. Add the egg and vanilla.
4. Add the flour to make a dough. If the dough feels a bit sticky, add a little bit more flour.
5. Once you have a dough, roll it out with a rolling pin so it is about 1cm thick.
6. Cut biscuits out into heart shapes and put on the baking sheet.
7. Put in the oven to cook for 8-10 minutes.
8. Mix icing sugar with water and food colouring to make a thick paste.
9. When cool, ice biscuits and add edible eyes.

DEVOTION 5

Thankfulness peacock

DEVOTION 7

Paper chains and bunting

DEVOTION 8

Cereal box picture frame

Praise Party

Praise Party

thank you prayers

Thank you, God, for praise parties!

Thank you for my great friends.

Thank you that I can dance.

Thank you that I can jump up high.

Thank you for my crazy arms.

Thank you for music that makes me spin.

Thank you for my swinging hips.

Thank you that I can praise You.

Thank you for my clapping hands.

Thank you, God, for my little worship time!

Amen.

Wonderful Day

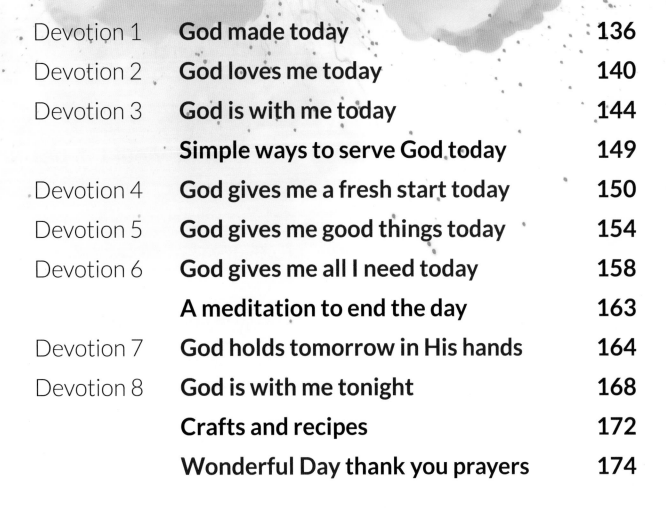

Psalm 118:24 (LWC)

This is the day that the Lord has made. Let us rejoice and be glad in it.

OK, Mum, I'm WIDE AWAKE! What are we going to do today?

Well, Hal... we're going to talk to God, and enjoy God's world, and show people God's love... It's going to be so much fun!

If you could choose one thing to do today, what would it be? A trip to the park? Or the seaside? Would you go out for a milkshake or have a picnic? Maybe you'd like to spend the day playing with your friends. There's so much to look forward to every day. And God has something amazing planned too!

The Bible says that God made today – that today is *His* wonderful day. And He wants to share it with us. God has a special plan for us today. Today, God wants us to find out a little bit more about Him. **Today, He wants us to see Him and love Him more.** And when we do, every day becomes an exciting adventure with God!

TALK TOGETHER

The Bible says that we should enjoy His special day. Talk about all the things that bring you joy each day – for example, your favourite places, people or toys. Say thank you to God for them.

MAKE TOGETHER

God made today. Make a picture frame out of lolly sticks with today's Bible verse or a picture of a sunrise inside. When you wake up every morning, look at your picture frame to remind you that today is God's day. Why not start each day saying the prayer below?

PRAY TOGETHER

Dear God, **thank you that You made today!** Thank you that I can enjoy today. Help me to see You and know You, today and every day. **Amen.**

Wonderful Day

1 TIME TO REFLECT

Psalm 118:19-24

Open for me the gates of the righteous; I will enter and give thanks to the Lord.
This is the gate of the Lord through which the righteous may enter.
I will give you thanks, for you answered me; you have become my salvation.

The stone the builders rejected has become the cornerstone;
the Lord has done this, and it is marvellous in our eyes.
The Lord has done it this very day; let us rejoice today and be glad.

"This is the day the Lord has made. Let us rejoice and be glad in it." This is more than a sweet sentiment. It's a victory cry – a call to celebration because God has done something *"marvellous in our eyes"*. The miraculous delivery at the heart of Psalm 118 was most likely Israel's triumph over their enemies in a specific battle. The king is leading his people in praise, entering the gates of Jerusalem on a day of celebration and thanksgiving. But there are forward echoes of a much bigger victory. Jesus himself quotes this psalm, calling himself the *"stone the builders rejected"* (verse 22) who becomes the cornerstone – the defining piece – of something amazing God is doing. God's ultimate victory is in defeating the powers of sin and death, leading His dearly-beloved people into new life with Him through Jesus.

And this ancient cry calls to us today too. The reality of most mornings is to get up and throw ourselves into the hundreds of things on our 'to-do' list before breakfast. But Psalm 118 reminds us of some important things as the day begins. Firstly – that we can have confidence in God today. Whatever surprises today may hold, we can rejoice in God's supreme victory – that because of Jesus, nothing can separate us from Him or His love. And it also reminds us that God is doing something marvellous today.

GOD'S BIG SALVATION PLAN IS A WORK IN PROGRESS. HE IS BRINGING NEW LIFE TO OUR WORLD, ONE HEART AT A TIME.

And the day ahead of us is our chance to join in with what God is doing – sharing His love, peace and hope with those around us.

TIME TO ACT

1 Read over these words from Romans 8: 37-39:

We are more than conquerors through him who loved us... Neither death nor life, neither angels nor demons, neither the present nor the future, nor any powers, neither height nor depth, nor anything else in all creation, will be able to separate us from the love of God that is in Christ Jesus our Lord.

Thank God that, as you journey through today, you are safe in His amazing love. You might want to rewrite the passage in your own words, including any issues that are close to your heart.

2 Psalm 118:24 reminds us that today is God's day. It's helpful to commit each day to God as it begins – although this can sometimes feel easier said than done! Perhaps you could stick Psalm 118:24 onto the fridge or tea tin and declare it as you make your morning cuppa. As you do, pray that God will use you for his glory today.

TIME TO PRAY

Father God,
I declare that today is Your day.

Give me ears to hear what You are saying and eyes to see what You are doing.

Make my hands quick to do Your work
and my feet quick to follow where You lead –
for Your eternal glory.

Amen.

---

60 SECONDS

ONLY GOT A MINUTE?

- Today is God's day and He journeys with us.

- Whatever surprises today may hold, you are safe in God's amazing love.

- God is doing something marvellous today and He invites you to join Him.

- This is our chance to join in with what God is doing and to share His love, peace and hope with those around us.

3 John 1:2 (LWC)

I pray that you are happy and healthy...

Hey, Dad. Can I pray that we have a fun day today?

Of course, Hal! And I pray that you will know just HOW MUCH God loves you today!

How do you feel when you wake up in the morning? Some days, you feel really excited. You can't wait to go out and run around! On other days, you'd rather stay indoors and play quietly. We can feel different things on different days. But whatever kind of day it is, and however we're feeling, we can be sure that God loves us.

The Bible says that we are special to God and that He really cares for us. And whether it's a sunny day or a rainy one, God is just the same. He doesn't have good days and grumpy days. **He's the same big, strong, loving, listening God who's with us every single day.** And He wants the very best for us today.

TALK TOGETHER

The best days are the ones spent with our favourite people! Talk about the people who are most special to you. What do you love about them? Thank God that you are precious to Him – and that He loves to be with you.

MAKE TOGETHER

God is just the same whether it's spring, summer, autumn or winter. Create a tree collage using real twigs and finger painting. Paint the leaves in different colours, or leave the twigs empty, to show the trees at different times of the year. Remember that God loves you just the same every day, all year round.

PRAY TOGETHER

Dear God, **thank you that whether it's a sunny day or a rainy day, You're just the same.** Thank you that You promise to love me, today and every day. **Amen.**

Wonderful Day

LITTLE

TIME TO REFLECT

3 John 1:1-4

The elder,
To my dear friend Gaius, whom I love in the truth.

Dear friend, I pray that you may enjoy good health and that all may go well with you, just as you are progressing spiritually. It gave me great joy when some believers came and testified about your faithfulness to the truth, telling how you continue to walk in it. I have no greater joy than to hear that my children are walking in the truth.

One of the remarkable privileges we have as God's children is prayer. God invites us to come to Him with our requests – and He listens. The Bible helpfully records a number of prayers. And this small snippet from John's letter to Gaius gives us an insight into the kinds of things Jesus' beloved disciple prayed for. Firstly, he prays that his friend would have good health. He also prays that things would generally go well with him. This probably sounds rather familiar.

MOST OF US STRIVE TO MAKE PRAYER A PART OF OUR DAILY ROUTINE – FOR OUR FAMILY, FOR OUR FRIENDS, FOR OURSELVES.

And, like John, our prayers probably revolve around these same themes. We pray that our children will be safe and well. We pray for the 'big thing' coming up at work. We pray for our friend's healing. And it's right and good that we pray for all of these things.

But John prays for something else too. Implicitly, He prays for Gaius' spiritual health – that his soul does well. This poses an interesting question for our own prayer time. How often do we pray for spiritual health? That we – and those around us – encounter God in the ins and outs and ups and downs of daily life? It's possible that God has a bigger plan for us today than just making sure the day passes without a problem: that what He ultimately wants is for us to know, trust and follow Him whatever we may be going through. As with Gaius, God takes delight in our faithfulness to Him. Perhaps praying that we learn to recognise God's own faithfulness to us today is a good place to begin.

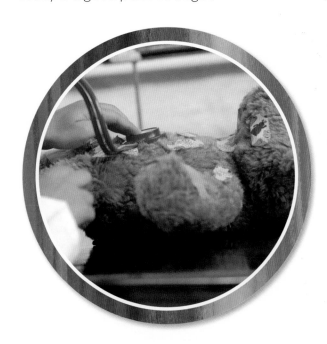

TIME TO ACT

1   Lamentations 3:22-23 says:

Because of the LORD's great love we are not consumed, for his compassions never fail.
They are new every morning; great is your faithfulness.

Take some time to list all the things that God has already given you today – whether that's material things, like a roof over your head, or spiritual blessings, like hope in Jesus. Use this to praise Him.

2   Spend some time praying for your children. Make your focus today their spiritual health and relationship with God. Try to spend some time listening to God, as well as talking to Him.

TIME TO PRAY

Father God, thank you that You always have time to listen to me.

Thank you that You care for me.

Help me to see and celebrate Your great faithfulness to me, that I may be faithful to You in turn – for Your eternal glory.

Amen.

ONLY GOT A MINUTE?

- God invites us to come to Him with our requests – and He listens.

- What are we currently praying for?

- God loves it when we pray, but how can we think bigger with our prayers?

- Do we just want our problems solved or do we want to know God in what we are going through?

- What might God want to say to us today?

DEVOTION 2 GREAT IS THY FAITHFULNESS

Wonderful Day

James 4:8 (LWC)

Be close to God and He will be close to you.

Mum, where is God? Is He at the park?

God is everywhere, Hal! Wherever you go, He'll always be by your side.

Who do you like to share your day with? Perhaps you have a favourite toy that comes with you wherever you go. Perhaps you love being with your family or your best friend. There's someone else who loves to be with us every day too – and that's God!

The Bible promises that God is always with us. And He loves it when we share our day with Him. We can do this by praying to Him. Praying is talking to God, just like we talk to our friends. We can tell Him about the things that make us happy. We can tell Him about the things which bother us as well. Wherever we are, He's always there to listen. And He cares for us more than we'll ever know!

TALK TOGETHER

The Bible says that God gives us His peace every day. Peace is a calm feeling we get when we know God is with us and helping us. Think about times in the day when you might want to feel God's peace.

MAKE TOGETHER

In the Bible, doves are a sign of God's peace. Make a dove using your handprint. Draw round your hand. Put a couple of eyes on the thumb, and the fingers will make the wings. Remember that God is with you in whatever you face today – and He gives you His peace.

PRAY TOGETHER

Dear God, **thank you that You promise to always be with me.** Thank you that I can talk to You about everything I do and everything I feel, today and every day. Amen.

LITTLE

TIME TO REFLECT

James 4:4-8a

You adulterous people, don't you know that friendship with the world means enmity against God? Therefore, anyone who chooses to be a friend of the world becomes an enemy of God. Or do you think Scripture says without reason that he jealously longs for the spirit he has caused to dwell in us? But he gives us more grace. That is why Scripture says:

'God opposes the proud but shows favour to the humble.'

Submit yourselves, then, to God. Resist the devil, and he will flee from you. Come near to God and he will come near to you.

God is with us. Four small words... one mind-blowing concept. It speaks of God's amazing love for us – that He sees us and walks beside us. It speaks of God's wonderful care for us – that He offers us His strength and peace in whatever we face. But James' words indicate that there is a two-way dynamic in play. God is not 'tagging along' with us each day – there in case of an emergency. He's inviting us into relationship with Him. James says, *"Come near to God and He will come near to you."* We are to be 'with God' as much as He is 'with us'.

What does this look like in real terms? Certainly, carving out regular time for God is a helpful practice – to hear what God might have to say to us each day. This is often easier said than done! It may be that we need to find new ways of keeping our daily channel to God 'open' during this busy, demanding season. But 'coming near' is more than this. In context, it seems to mean 'choosing' God – making Him Lord of our daily decisions. Every day we face a thousand subtle temptations to put our pride and our interests over obedience – from how we treat each other, to our relationship with money.

"COMING NEAR", THEN, IS THE AGE-OLD CALL TO LOVE GOD WITH HEART, SOUL, MIND AND STRENGTH.

God's love for us is never in question. He is with us and for us. But it's only as we in turn say "yes" to God each day that we can fully receive all He has to give us.

TIME TO ACT

1 There are many ways of encountering God during the day, beyond the traditional 'quiet time'. You can talk to God while out and about. Combine routine tasks with playing and singing worship music or stick Bible verses around your house to remind you of God's promises.

2 In his letter, James suggests that there is a spiritual battle raging each day. Take some time to reflect on any weak points you might have. Are there any temptations you face each day? Talk to God about them. Claim His promise to give you His presence, peace and protection in these critical moments.

TIME TO PRAY

Father God, thank you that You promise to be with me each day.

I choose to be with You today too – to draw near to You and honour You in all that I say and do, for Your eternal glory.

Amen.

60 SECONDS

ONLY GOT A MINUTE?

- God is with us.
- God is not 'tagging along' with us but is inviting us into relationship with Him.
- Coming near to God means choosing Him and rechoosing Him, again and again.
- It is only as we say "yes" to God each day that we can fully receive all He has to give us.

Wonderful Day

Joshua 24:15

As for me and my household, we will **serve the Lord.**

"Be happy and do good"
SIMPLE WAYS TO SERVE GOD TODAY

Ecclesiastes 3:12 says that "there is nothing better for people than to be happy and to do good". Every day is full of opportunities to help others – something that pleases God and, more often than not, adds to our own happiness. Here are some thoughts to get you and your family started. Can you think of any others?

- **Practise hospitality.** Open your home to others. It could be a visiting student from overseas, an elderly neighbour or your children's friends. Invite them round for a cuppa or a meal.

- **Be welcoming.** Something as simple as chatting to somebody who's new or by themselves can make a huge difference to their day! Make it a regular family challenge. Whether you're at work, at school or at playgroup, can you make someone smile today?

- **Make a blessing bin.** Keep a basket or box around the house. Add things to it as and when – clothes that are too small, toys that are no longer played with – or even any chocolates you find on offer at the supermarket. Then when you see someone in need of blessing, you'll be ready!

- **Love your neighbour.** Drop a meal round to someone in need – whether that's someone with a new baby, or a sick or elderly neighbour. Be aware of any practical needs that anyone in the street might have – especially the most vulnerable. How could you help them?

- **Talk about giving.** Research charities which you could support as a family, from local night shelters to overseas child sponsorship. Find ways for all the family to play a part – for example, by organising a simple sponsored activity.

- **Party!** Whatever the occasion – Christmas, bonfire night, or just a lovely summer's day – host a party for your street to get to know and love your neighbours.

- **Be kind.** Why not run a family 'act of kindness' challenge? See if you can do one kind act every day for a week, whether that's writing kind notes or pictures, or baking cakes for work colleagues.

- **Support your local food bank.** Pick up one or two items whenever you do the weekly shop. Take a child-friendly shopping list with you (i.e. with pictures, not words). Invite your children to choose what they'd like to donate.

- **Support social action projects.** Some churches run days where they help the local community. Sign up and serve as a family.

- **Babysit for free.** A couple of easy evenings out for Mum and Dad can work wonders for the whole family! Who could you bless with the gift of babysitting?

I got cross and now I feel sad. I really messed up.

1 John 1:19 (LWC)

If we say sorry to God when we get something wrong, we can be sure that He will always, always make it right again.

Don't worry, Hal. God can make it better. Just tell Him all about it.

Sometimes, days don't turn out well. We might have said things we didn't mean and made people sad. We might have broken something. We might have been cross with someone or had someone be cross with us. It can leave us unhappy with our day and feeling sad that we messed up. If this is the case, it's OK!

The Bible says that God really loves us. He knows all about the mistakes we make – nothing surprises Him! He also sees our heart and knows when we are sorry for the bad choices we make. When we say sorry to Him, He forgives us and gives us another chance. No matter what kind of mess we might make today, **God lets us begin again – just as if it never happened.**

TALK TOGETHER

Sometimes we can make bad choices and do things which make God and other people sad. Can you think of any examples? Think about how God promises to forgive us when we say sorry – and about how He can help us to make good choices in future that will make Him smile.

MAKE TOGETHER

God cleans up our mess! Make some cleaning liquid using lemon juice and water and clean your house with a grown-up! Thank God that our own mess isn't the end of the story.

PRAY TOGETHER

Dear God, **thank you that whatever I do, You still love me.** I'm sorry for the times when I make a mess and hurt other people. Thank you that You promise to give me a second chance, today and every day. **Amen.**

Wonderful Day

TIME TO REFLECT

1 John 1:8-2:2

If we claim to be without sin, we deceive ourselves and the truth is not in us. If we confess our sins, he is faithful and just and will forgive us our sins and purify us from all unrighteousness. If we claim we have not sinned, we make him out to be a liar and his word is not in us.

My dear children, I write this to you so that you will not sin. But if anybody does sin, we have an advocate with the Father – Jesus Christ, the Righteous One. He is the atoning sacrifice for our sins, and not only for ours but also for the sins of the whole world.

Some days don't feel so wonderful. The morning begins with so much promise. But as the day progresses, things go awry. At breakfast time, there isn't enough milk for everyone to have cereal. One child takes forever to eat their toast. Another refuses to get dressed. By nine o'clock, you're running late, having already ruined the perfect day ahead by being cross with the kids. We can blame whatever we like.Sleep deprivation. Stress. Other people. But although these might exacerbate matters, in our heart of hearts we know what the real problem is: our sin. We are not as good, as patient or as loving as we should be. And so often it leaves us feeling like we've failed our family, ourselves – and ultimately God.

But this needn't define our day – or our lives. We often think of confession in negative terms. Nobody likes to admit that they're wrong. When we make mistakes, our instinct is to carry on, vowing to do better next time. But this only leaves us carrying the consequences of our sin, and bearing the weight of our brokenness.

IN THE BIBLE, CONFESSION IS SEEN AS A WONDERFUL, POSITIVE EXPERIENCE — A WAY OF RECEIVING GOD'S GRACE.

John writes that it's inevitable that we will mess up. It's a sad condition of our fallen humanity. But God knows our weakness – and He loves us anyway. We will have days when everything seems to go wrong. But God in His mercy has already made it right, in Jesus. There are second, third, infinite chances available to us each day. And when we learn to say sorry – to God and each other – we find that we can finally enjoy the freedom that forgiveness brings.

TIME TO ACT

1   There are many occasions in the day when we make messy and mucky things clean again – for example, washing dirty dishes, the laundry, the kitchen worktop and ourselves. As you do any of these today, confess your sins to God, being confident that He forgives us and makes us new.

2   James writes that we should confess our sins to one another (James 5:16). You might want to find somebody you trust to whom you can be accountable, as a way of helping you become the person God is making you to be.

TIME TO PRAY

Father God,
Thank you that You are faithful and just.

Thank you that You will forgive us our sins and purify us from all unrighteousness – for Your eternal glory.

Amen.

ONLY GOT A MINUTE?

- Failure doesn't need to define us.

- We will mess up, but God knows our weakness and loves us anyway.

- God in His mercy has already made it right through Jesus.

- Confession allows us to receive God's grace.

- When we say sorry, we can find true freedom and forgiveness.

Wonderful Day

I love playing in the garden! It's so much fun!

Ecclesiastes 3:11

He has made everything beautiful in its time.

Me too, Hal. God gives us so many wonderful things every day. Isn't He great?

What are the best bits of your day? Perhaps it's playing with favourite toys at home or going out to special places. Maybe it's laughing with your family or friends. Maybe it's eating your pudding! There are all kinds of wonderful things to enjoy every day. And the Bible says that they're all gifts from God.

The Bible says that God has made all things beautiful. He gives us good things each day, from the food we eat, to our family and friends – even the sunshine, the trees and the flowers around us! So, whatever you do today that makes you feel happy or excited, remember to say a great BIG thank you to the One who made it happen – God!

TALK TOGETHER

Talk about what has made you happy today. It might be something you did, or someone or something you saw. Or it might be something you ate! Thank God for all of these wonderful things.

MAKE TOGETHER

God fills every day with good things! Why not make some good things yourself? Bake some chocolate cereal cakes, then why not share them with others? As you eat them, thank God for all the wonderful things He gives you every day. **See the recipe on page 172.**

PRAY TOGETHER

Dear God, **thank you that You love me so much.** Thank you that You give me lots and lots of good things, today and every day! **Amen.**

Wonderful Day

LITTLE

TIME TO REFLECT

Ecclesiastes 3:9-13

What do workers gain from their toil? I have seen the burden God has laid on the human race. He has made everything beautiful in its time. He has also set eternity in the human heart; yet no one can fathom what God has done from beginning to end. I know that there is nothing better for people than to be happy and to do good while they live. That each of them may eat and drink, and find satisfaction in all their toil – this is the gift of God.

Carpe diem **– seize the day.** Or, to give it a 21st century spin, YOLO – You Only Live Once. For millennia, people have been told to make the most of the life they've been given. But the reality of our daily experience is rather more mundane. We get up and begin the day's chores. We rush from one place to the next, one task to the next, until we crash into bedtime, barely able to remember what we've done all day. If we're ever tempted to wonder if life is passing us by, these words from Ecclesiastes offer a refreshing perspective. They were written by a man who was renowned in his lifetime for his extraordinary achievements. And his best advice for a life well lived is simply to find enjoyment and satisfaction in the midst of the ordinary and everyday – from the food we eat, to the people in our lives, to our daily work.

For, the teacher declares, God "has made everything beautiful in its time". These words serve as a reminder to slow down – to appreciate the many good things which, in our busyness, we can miss or take for granted.

EVERY DAY IS FULL OF GIFTS FROM GOD. AND AS WE ENJOY THEM, WITH THANKSGIVING, WE ENCOUNTER GOD.

But these words can be read as a promise too. They sit in a chapter that reminds us that life passes through different seasons (Ecclesiastes 3:1-8). Seasons of joy and energy. Seasons of sorrow and weariness. But whatever the season, God can – and will – make it beautiful. Each day offers a new opportunity to experience His faithfulness – yes, even during the hard times. We just need to take each day as it comes – and give it humbly to God.

TIME TO ACT

1   Ecclesiastes reminds us that we go through good times and hard times. Raising young children can feel like both the greatest and toughest time of our life all at once. Take some time to write down words that sum up this season for you. Give them to God. How has He made/is He making this season beautiful?

2   One very practical way of finding enjoyment and satisfaction each day is to eat together round the table as a family, without distractions. Try to build this into your daily routine. Take turns to share some of the things you've enjoyed from the day and be thankful for them.

TIME TO PRAY

Father God, thank you that You have made everything beautiful in its time.

Thank you for the many wonderful gifts that You give me every day.

Help me to see You each day, whichever season I am in – for Your eternal glory.

Amen.

60 SECONDS

ONLY GOT A MINUTE?

- Slow down.
- Every day is full of gifts from God. As we rush around, we can miss them.
- Right now, which gifts has God given you to enjoy?
- There are seasons of sorrow and weariness, but in every season God has promised that He will bring beauty.
- Give your day to God. Which gifts is He giving you today?

Wonderful Day

2 Corinthians 9:8 (LWC)

God is able to give you all you need – and more!

Hey Dad, I'm SO thirsty! Please could I have a drink?

Of course, Hal. I'll always give you what you need. And so will God.

There are all sorts of things that we need every day. Sometimes these are things we can see and touch – like food to eat and clothes to wear. Sometimes we need things that we can't see, but they're just as important. We might need courage to do something difficult. Or we might need a friend to talk to.

Jesus said that we should ask God for our 'daily bread'. It's Jesus' way of describing all the things we need each day. The Bible promises that God will give us whatever we need and more. We just need to ask Him. So if there's something that you need today, or something you're worried about, talk to God about it. **It's amazing what He will do!**

TALK TOGETHER

Talk about some of the things you need every day. Think about things you can see and touch – and the things you can't, like courage. Is there anything you might need today or this week? Ask God for it!

MAKE TOGETHER

God gives us our daily bread – in other words, everything we need each day. Bake some bread rolls with your family or friends. As you eat them, thank God that He will always give us everything we need! **See the recipe on page 173.**

PRAY TOGETHER

Dear God, **thank you that You care for me so much.** Thank you that You promise to give me everything that I need, today and every day. **Amen.**

TIME TO REFLECT

2 Corinthians 9:8-11

And God is able to bless you abundantly, so that in all things at all times, having all that you need, you will abound in every good work. As it is written:

'They have freely scattered their gifts to the poor; their righteousness endures for ever.'

Now he who supplies seed to the sower and bread for food will also supply and increase your store of seed and will enlarge the harvest of your righteousness. You will be enriched in every way so that you can be generous on every occasion, and through us your generosity will result in thanksgiving to God.

George Müller was a hero of the faith who grabbed hold of God's promise to meet our daily needs with both hands. Living in Bristol, England, in the 1800s, Müller built great orphanages, and in his lifetime cared for over 10,000 of the city's poorest children. What's remarkable is that he never asked anybody for a single penny to fund the work – only God. His diaries track his developing faith in God's provision. When George Müller was a young minister, money was tight. He and his wife often didn't know where the next meal would be coming from. But he'd pray – and provisions would appear. Müller records in his diary how on one occasion, just as the cupboards emptied, a steady stream of visitors dropped by with groceries – including luxuries like chocolate and coffee – and money to purchase the rest! God literally provided their daily bread, and more.

TIME AND AGAIN THE BIBLE REPEATS THIS TREMENDOUS PROMISE — THAT GOD WILL PROVIDE.

He is our good Father. Whatever we need each day, we simply need to ask for it. But there's an interesting context to this promise. Paul's words to the Corinthians are part and parcel of a call to live generously. Jesus' famous words in Matthew 6:33 that *"all these things [i.e. food, clothes] will be given to you"* follow a command to *"seek first his kingdom"*. Seen from this perspective, God is not a divine vending machine so much as the Kingdom CEO, liberally covering our expenses. At its heart, this promise is an assurance that we will never be short-changed by God. And as we commit ourselves to God each day, to love and serve Him with generous hearts, we can be confident that He'll put all the resources of heaven at our disposal.

TIME TO ACT

1 What do you need today? It might be something material, emotional or spiritual. Ask God for it now. It might help to write it down – and then keep a record of God's answer to your prayers.

2 God's provision comes as we give all we have to Him. Is there something God might be challenging you to give to Him? Your talents? Your time? Your resources?

TIME TO PRAY

Father God, thank you that
You are my Father in heaven.

Thank you that You are so incredibly generous to me, and that You promise to meet my needs every day.

May I learn what it means to give as You give – for Your eternal glory.

Amen.

60 SECONDS

ONLY GOT A MINUTE?

- God will provide.

- Whatever we need each day, we simply need to ask for it.

- As a response to His generosity, God calls us to be generous.

- Commit yourself to God each day. Love and serve Him with a generous heart.

- Be confident that He will put all the resources of heaven at your disposal to carry out His good work.

Trust in the LORD
with all your heart,
and lean not on
your own understanding;
in all your ways
submit to Him,
and He will make
your paths straight.

Proverbs
3:5-6

Before you go to bed...

A MEDITATION TO END THE DAY

Think about all the good things you have experienced today.

Think about where you have seen God at work,

The times when you have felt His presence.

Think about the times when God has used you today for His glory.

Say thank you to God.

Think about the times you have struggled today.

Think about the times your words or actions
haven't lived up to God's perfect will.

Say sorry to God.

Picture yourself holding all the events of the day.

Is there anything that you are finding hard to carry?

Something which is hurting you to hold onto?

Or something you are worried you might drop?

Give it to God.

Look ahead to tomorrow.

Pray that you will see God more,

Know God more,

Love God more –

For His eternal glory.

Wonderful Day

Psalm 46:10

Be still and know that I am God.

I had fun today, Mum. But I'm a bit worried about tomorrow.

That's OK, Hal. Why don't we tell God all about it?

So you've had a busy day. And at bedtime there are lots of things buzzing around in your head. It's always nice to go to sleep thinking about the fun things we've done. But sometimes, things happen in the day that upset us. Or we know it's going to be a big day tomorrow. On these nights, we may go to bed feeling a bit worried.

In the Bible, God says: "Be still and know that I am God". He's saying that we can feel completely calm because He's amazing and there's nothing He can't do. And what's more, He really, really loves us. So as we go to bed, let's give every bit of today and tomorrow to God, knowing that He takes care of everything – including us!

TALK TOGETHER

Sometimes we can feel worried about things which have happened during the day – or about something that might happen tomorrow. Can you think of any examples? Is there anything you want to talk to God about now?

MAKE TOGETHER

We don't need to worry – God's in charge! Make a night light by decorating a jam jar with tissue paper. Put a little LED light inside, which you can leave on at bedtime. When you go to sleep, look at the light and remember that God is in control of tomorrow.

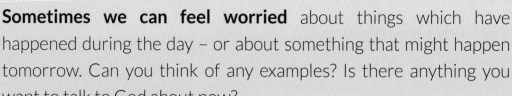

PRAY TOGETHER

Dear God, **thank you that You are bigger than everything in this world.** Thank you that I don't need to worry about anything, because You're in charge – today and every day. **Amen.**

Wonderful Day

TIME TO REFLECT

Psalm 46

God is our refuge and strength, an ever-present help in trouble.
Therefore we will not fear, though the earth give way and the mountains fall into the heart of the sea, though its waters roar and foam and the mountains quake with their surging.
There is a river whose streams make glad the city of God, the holy place where the Most High dwells. God is within her, she will not fall; God will help her at break of day.
Nations are in uproar, kingdoms fall; he lifts his voice, the earth melts.

The Lord Almighty is with us; the God of Jacob is our fortress.

Come and see what the Lord has done, the desolations he has brought on the earth.
He makes wars cease to the ends of the earth.
He breaks the bow and shatters the spear; he burns the shields with fire.
He says, 'Be still, and know that I am God; I will be exalted among the nations,
I will be exalted in the earth.'
The Lord Almighty is with us; the God of Jacob is our fortress.

The Bible is full of commands. And the one which occurs most often is *"do not be afraid"*. This is worth noting because fear, anxiety and worry are emotions which probably feature quite high up on our list of daily experiences. On a personal level, there's a lot we may worry about. We harbour fears around our health, our work, our family and our finances. The same is true on a national or global scale. We listen to the news, warning about the state of the environment, the economy, relations between countries and everything besides. During the day, worry can follow us about, snapping at our heels. And in the wee small hours of the night, our fears often loom large.

There's no denying that life can be hard. There are lots of serious issues we face each day, many of which are out of our hands. But passages like Psalm 46 offer us reassurance and peace. They remind us again of the God we serve: our refuge and strength. A word from Him can calm the chaos: *"Be still and know that I am God."* This command to 'be still' is echoed later in Jesus' commands to the wind and waves (Mark 4:39) – a wonderful picture of how nothing is beyond God's power, and nobody beyond His love. This same command to *"be still"* speaks to us too.

WHATEVER WE FACE — WHATEVER STORMS RAGE IN OUR OWN LIVES, OR IN THE LIFE OF OUR NATION OR WORLD — GOD IS GREATER THAN THEM ALL.

And as uncertain and unpredictable as life can seem, we can find rest in the Eternal God who gives *"strength for today and bright hope for tomorrow"**.

*Thomas Obediah Chisholm
© 1951 Hope Publishing Company

TIME TO ACT

1   Meditate on these words from Psalm 46:

God is our refuge and strength,
an ever-present help in trouble.

Reflect on each word in turn:

***God** is our refuge…*

*God **is** our refuge…*

*God is **our** refuge…* and so on.

Thank God for this wonderful promise to us.

2   There's so much we don't know about the day ahead, the week ahead and the years ahead. But as the saying goes, we may not know what the future holds, but we know who holds the future. Take some time to pray into some of the big things facing you, your family and your nation at this time.

TIME TO PRAY

Father God,
Thank you that You are my refuge and my strength, an ever-present help in trouble.

Thank you that I can be still,
knowing that You are God today and every day –
to Your eternal glory.

Amen.

60 SECONDS

ONLY GOT A MINUTE?

- God commands us to *"be still"*.

- To be still means to cease striving and worrying, and simply to acknowledge who God is.

- Whatever we face, and whatever storms rage, God is greater than them all.

- We can find rest in the Eternal God, the same yesterday, today and forever.

Wonderful Day

Proverbs 3:24 (LWC)

When you go to bed, you will **not be scared.**

When you lie down, your **sleep** will be **sweet.**

Yawn... I feel really tired...

It's time to say goodnight, Hal. But remember – we're not far away. And neither is God!

It's the end of the day. Maybe you're tucked up in bed already. It feels warm and cosy. Soon your mummy or daddy or another favourite grown-up will say goodnight. But sometimes, when they leave, we feel a bit sad. We might not like suddenly being alone in the dark.

If you ever feel that way, here's some happy news. The Bible promises that God isn't going anywhere! God is with you when you wake up. He's beside you during the day. And He's still with you at bedtime. The Bible says that God watches over us day and night. So, as we drift off to sleep, let's know that God is right beside us – **our big Heavenly Dad and our best friend!**

TALK
TOGETHER

How many of God's promises to us can you remember? What do they mean to you? Thank God for His awesome promises!

MAKE
TOGETHER

We don't need to be worried – God is with us! Make a sign to hang on your door. Ask a grown-up to write 'God is with me'. Decorate it with your favourite stickers and colours. Look at it at bedtime, and know that God is beside you as you sleep.

PRAY
TOGETHER

Dear God, **thank you that I never need to be afraid because You love me SO much.** Thank you that You promise to watch over me, today and every day. **Amen.**

TIME TO REFLECT

Proverbs 3:21-24

*My son, do not let wisdom and understanding out of your sight,
preserve sound judgment and discretion;
they will be life for you, an ornament to grace your neck.*

Then you will go on your way in safety, and your foot will not stumble.

When you lie down, you will not be afraid; when you lie down, your sleep will be sweet.

It isn't only the things we can't control that have the power to keep us up at night. Sometimes it's the things that are in our hands that cause us anxiety. A parenting issue with our children. A problem that needs resolving in a relationship. A decision that will have repercussions for our family's future. Every day, we face situations that demand we take decisive action. And we're often left asking ourselves, "Am I doing the right thing?" Yet the Bible regularly promises that we can enjoy sweet sleep, free of worry. The secret to a good night's rest is found in God. It's not just that He is with us in every situation we face. It's that – once again – when we make loving Him our life's primary concern, He promises to manage the rest.

Seeking God's wisdom lies at the heart of this. The writer of Proverbs says that *"the fear of the Lord is the beginning of wisdom"* (Proverbs 9:10). A good question to ask in a difficult situation might be, "What does it look like to honour God in this situation?" Or more simply, "What would Jesus do?" – a question that's no less relevant for being so often used. At other times, perhaps we simply need to ask God for *"judgment and discernment"* (Proverbs 3:21) or, as

The Message translates it, *"clear thinking and common sense"*. Of all the wonderful resources God promises to give us in our daily lives, these rarely get a mention. But they're ours for the taking.

AND THE GOD WHO PROMISES TO HELP US IN ANY AND EVERY SITUATION PROMISES TO GIVE US HIS PEACE TONIGHT — AND ALWAYS.

TIME TO ACT

1　Take some time to pray into any situations you are facing or decisions that need making. Ask God to give you His wisdom. Do the same for your national leaders. Ask God to give them His wisdom and good judgment as they make decisions on behalf of your country.

2　Many of us have a tendency to try to manage things either by ourselves, or in a couple, and/or with God. But one of the blessings of being part of a church network is being able to add 'community' into the equation. Who are the trusted individuals around you who can offer practical wisdom, as well as support, in the difficult situations you might be facing today?

TIME TO PRAY

Father God, thank you for all Your good promises to me.

Thank you that You love me.

Thank you that You are with me.

Thank you that You give me good gifts and much-needed resources.

Thank you that You offer me Your wisdom and perfect peace.

Teach me to live in the light of Your extraordinary faithfulness to me today and always – for Your eternal glory.

Amen.

60 SECONDS

ONLY GOT A MINUTE?

- The secret to a good night's rest is found in God.

- When we make loving Him our primary concern, God promises to take care of everything else.

- God promises to help us in any and every situation, and He promises to give us His peace tonight – and always.

Wonderful Day

Crafts and recipes

DEVOTION 5   CHOCOLATE CEREAL CAKES

- 100g (4oz) chocolate
- 75g (3oz) cereal
- Cupcake cases

1. Break the chocolate into pieces and put in a heatproof glass bowl.

2. Sit the glass bowl on top of a saucepan filled with one third hot water.

3. Wait for the chocolate to melt.

4. When the chocolate has melted, take the glass bowl off the saucepan and put it on a heatproof mat. Warning – it will be hot!

5. Mix the cereal into the chocolate and stir.

6. Spoon into little cupcake cases.

7. Put in the fridge until set.

DEVOTION 1

Lolly stick picture frame

DEVOTION 2

Tree collage

DEVOTION 3

Handprint dove

DEVOTION 6 — BREAD ROLLS

- 500g (20oz) strong wholemeal bread flour
- 1½ tsp salt
- 1 tsp sugar
- 15g (½oz) butter (softened)
- 1 sachet easy bake yeast (7g)
- 300ml warm water
- Egg to glaze

1. Put flour, salt, sugar and yeast in a large bowl and add the butter, working it between your fingers to get breadcrumbs.
2. Add the water slowly to form a soft dough.
3. Knead the dough on a lightly floured surface until the dough is smooth and elastic.
4. Separate the dough into 8-10 balls.
5. Place the balls on a baking tray, cover and leave in a warm place for around 35-40 minutes, until the dough has risen and doubled in size.
6. Preheat the oven to 230°C/210°C fan/gas mark 8.
7. Brush the surface of the rolls with beaten egg.
8. Bake the rolls for 15 minutes, then reduce the oven temperature to 200°C (180°C/gas mark 6) for the final 10 minutes until the rolls are risen and golden brown. Check that they sound hollow when tapped underneath. Cool on a wire rack.

DEVOTION 4

Clean house

DEVOTION 7

Jam jar lantern

DEVOTION 8

Door sign

Wonderful Day

Thank you, God, for my really fun day!

Thank you
for the friends I have played with.

Thank you for all of my laughing.

Thank you
for the people who have looked after me.

Thank you for all of the playing.

Thank you for my family.

Thank you for the food I have eaten.

Thank you for my cosy bed.

Thank you for the dreams I will have.

Bless my sleep tonight,

Amen.

Also available from

Little WORSHIP Company

The **Little Worship Company** offers a range of inspiring products, including DVDs, an app **(Little Worship Company World)**, devotionals, curriculums and books. Our products are filled with beautifully-produced worship videos, prayers, games, stories and Bible quotes.

Each DVD follows a devotional journey, teaching your child timeless Bible truths. The DVDs and app have been created to help adults and children to discover God together at home, at church or out in the community.

✉ info@littleworshipcompany.com   f Littleworshipcompany   ⬛ @littleworshipcompany

Little Worship Company World

Worship anytime, anywhere

Through our digital world, hosted by the entertaining **Looyah family,** you and your child will be taken on a journey through beautifully-produced worship videos, games, stories, Bible quotes and age-appropriate studies. Each week there will be a new exciting journey of content to explore, as you and your little one discover God together.

 Download on the **App Store**    GET IT ON **Google Play**   Available at **amazon**

Our **home devotional guide** accompanies our **DVD collection**. The four DVDs: **Amazing Me, Beautiful World, Praise Party** and **Wonderful Day** help us to explore more about the God who made us and loves us. Join Hal and Mr. and Mrs. Looyah on an exciting journey with songs, Bible verses and lots of fun in this entertaining DVD series.

Little Worship Company DVD collection
At home

Now available to buy at littleworshipcompany.com/shop

Resources for church and outreach
At church

Our **church-licensed DVD and curriculum** creates opportunities for easy Sunday School and outreach activities. With multiple craft ideas and active games built on solid Bible foundations, there are instant lesson plans and family services created for you. All materials are suitable for a churched and unchurched audience with intergenerational appeal.